HUGH MACLENNAN'S *THE WATCH THAT ENDS THE NIGHT*

Canadian Fiction Studies

Margaret Laurence's *The Diviners* CFS 17
Louis Hémon's *Maria Chapdelaine* CFS 18
Lucy Maud Montgomery's *Anne of Green Gables* CFS 19
John Richardson's *Wacousta* CFS 20
Timothy Findley's *Not Wanted on the Voyage* CFS 21
Morley Callaghan's *The Loved and the Lost* CFS 22
Margaret Atwood's *Life Before Man* CFS 23
Margaret Laurence's *The Fire-Dwellers* CFS 24
Alice Munro's *Something I've Been Meaning to Tell You* CFS 25
Gabrielle Roy's *The Tin Flute* CFS 26
W.O. Mitchell's *Who Has Seen the Wind* CFS 27
Margaret Atwood's *Bodily Harm* CFS 28
Hugh MacLennan's *The Watch That Ends the Night* CFS 29
Joy Kogawa's *Obasan* CFS 30

Additional volumes are in preparation

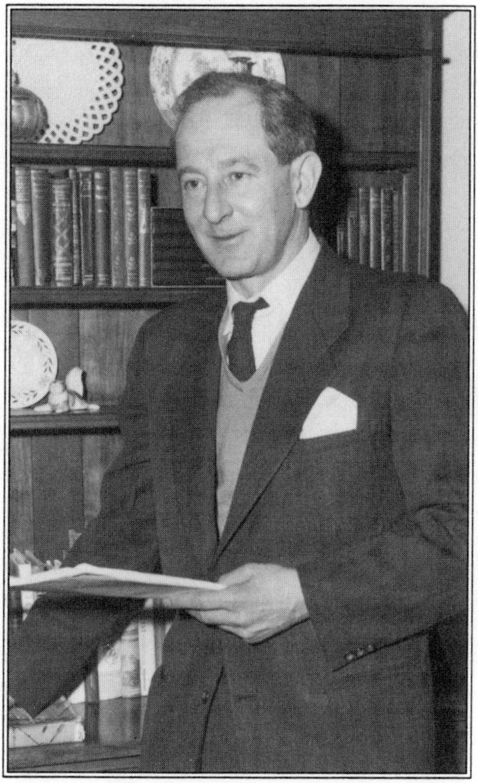

Life Struggle:
HUGH MACLENNAN'S
The Watch That Ends the Night

W.J. Keith

ECW PRESS

Copyright © ECW PRESS, 1993

CANADIAN CATALOGUING IN PUBLICATION DATA

Keith, W.J.
Life struggle : Hugh MacLennan's
The Watch That Ends the Night
(Canadian fiction studies ; no. 29)
Includes bibliographic references.
Includes index.
ISBN 1-55022-178-7

1. MacLennan, Hugh, 1907-1990. The Watch That
Ends the Night. I. Title. II. Series.

PS8523.A86J437 1993   C813.54   C90-094509-5
PR9199.3.L38J437 1993

This book has been published with the assistance of the
Ministry of Culture, Recreation and Tourism of the Province
of Ontario, through funds provided by the Ontario
Publishing Centre, and with the assistance of grants from
The Canada Council, the Ontario Arts Council, and the
Government of Canada through the Department of
Communications, and the Canadian Studies and Special Projects
Directorate of the Department of the Secretary of State of Canada.

The cover features a reproduction of the dust-wrapper
from the first edition of *The Watch That Ends the Night*, courtesy
of the Thomas Fisher Rare Book Library, University of Toronto.
Frontispiece photograph from the Montreal *Star*,
courtesy the National Archives of Canada.
Design and imaging by ECW Type & Art, Oakville, Ontario.
Printed and bound by Kromar Printing, Winnipeg, Manitoba.

Distributed by General Distribution Services,
30 Lesmill Road, Don Mills, Ontario M3B 2T6.

Published by ECW PRESS,
1980 Queen Street East,
Toronto, Ontario M4L 1J2.

Table of Contents

A Note on the Author 6
Chronology 9
The Importance of the Work 13
Critical Reception 17
Reading of the Text 26
   Approaches to the Text 26
      "This book is about . . ." 26
      Novel Versus Romance 30
      "The story of one's story" 33
      Time in the Novel: The Novel in Time 39
   Interpreting the Text 41
      Title and Dedication 42
      Part 1: Voices from the Past 46
      Part 2: The Ignominy of Boyhood 54
      Part 3: Casualties 60
      Part 4: Threatening Shadows 63
      Part 5: Dark Journey 71
      Part 6: A Low Dishonest Decade 76
      Part 7: The Courage To Be 86
      Epilogue: Into Mystery 95
Postscript: Hugh MacLennan and Robertson Davies . . 97
Works Cited 102
Index 107

☐ A Note on the Author ☐

W.J. Keith was born in England and graduated from Cambridge before emigrating to Canada in 1958 to pursue graduate studies in English at the University of Toronto. After gaining his Ph.D. in 1961, he taught for five years at McMaster University before returning to the University of Toronto, where he is now Professor of English at University College. Before turning his full attention to Canadian literary studies, he established himself with several books on the rural literature of England. His publications in Canadian literature include *Epic Fiction: The Art of Rudy Wiebe* (1981), *Canadian Literature in English* (1985), *A Sense of Style: Studies in the Art of Fiction in English-Speaking Canada* (1989), and an earlier volume in the present series, *Introducing Margaret Atwood's The Edible Woman* (1989). His most recent volumes are a collection of essays on Canadian criticism and fiction (including an essay on *The Watch That Ends the Night*), *An Independent Stance* (1991), and *Literary Images of Ontario* (1992). He was editor of the *University of Toronto Quarterly* between 1976 and 1985, and was elected Fellow of the Royal Society of Canada in 1979.

NOTE ON EDITIONS AND REFERENCES

The Watch That Ends the Night was originally published in Toronto by the Macmillan Company of Canada, in New York by Scribner's, and in London by Heinemann. All these editions have the same pagination. It was later published in reset editions by the New American Library in both Canada and the United States, and in England by Pan Books. In 1975, the novel was reprinted by Macmillan as a Laurentian Library paperback, which followed the pagination of the 1959 editions. In 1986 it appeared in the Macmillan Paperback series, and in 1991 in a paperback from General Publishing. All of these editions reproduce the original pagination; this is the text followed in the present study.

A substantial though incomplete typescript of "Requiem," the original title for *The Watch That Ends the Night*, is in the Thomas Fisher Rare Book Room of the University of Toronto Library. This appears to be the original version submitted to the Macmillan Company of Canada. It contains some cancelled passages, but lacks the final revisions. The best collection of MacLennan material is in the University of Calgary Library (see Jean F. Tener, *et al.*, *The Hugh MacLennan Papers*), but these holdings contain relatively little pertaining to this particular novel.

Life Struggle:
Hugh MacLennan's
The Watch That Ends the Night

Chronology

1907	John Hugh MacLennan born 20 March in Glace Bay, Nova Scotia, where his father was a doctor (an elder sister had been born in 1902).
1914	First World War begins.
1914–15	Family moves briefly to Sidney, Nova Scotia, and then settles in Halifax. Father serves for a short time in army.
1917	Halifax explosion, 6 December.
1918	End of First World War.
1924–28	Attends Dalhousie University, enrolling in Honours Latin and Greek. Graduates in 1928, winning a Governor General's Gold Medal for Classics and a Rhodes Scholarship.
1928–32	Studies Classics at Oriel College, Oxford, and travels widely on the European continent.
1929	Wall Street crash, 24 October, precipitates the Great Depression.
1932	B.A. Oxford.
1932–35	Doctoral student in Classics at Princeton.
1933	Nazis come to power in Germany under Hitler.
1935	Ph.D. Princeton, in Roman history. Thesis published as first book, *Oxyrhynchus: An Economic and Social Study*. Becomes teacher of Latin and History at Lower Canada College, Montreal.
1936	Marries Dorothy Duncan, an American writer and (subsequently) painter. Spanish Civil War begins.
1937	Accompanies tour to the Soviet Union.

1939	Death of father. End of Spanish Civil War with victory of General Franco. Second World War begins.
1941	*Barometer Rising* (novel).
1944	Dorothy Duncan publishes *Partner in Three Worlds* (winner of Governor-General's Award for non-fiction).
1945	*Two Solitudes* (novel). Leaves Lower Canada College to begin freelance literary career. End of Second World War and beginning of atomic age.
1946	Wins Governor-General's Award for *Two Solitudes*.
1948	*The Precipice* (novel; also winner of Governor-General's Award).
1949	*Cross-Country* (prose; Governor-General's Award for non-fiction).
1950	Korean War begins.
1951	*Each Man's Son* (novel). Becomes part-time teacher of English at McGill University.
1952	University of New Brunswick bestows on MacLennan the first of his many honorary degrees. Wins Lorne Pierce Medal from the Royal Society of Canada.
1953	End of Korean War. Elected Fellow of the Royal Society of Canada.
1954	*Thirty and Three* (essays, ed. Dorothy Duncan; Governor-General's Award for non-fiction).
1956	Elected Fellow of the Royal Society of Literature.
1957	Dorothy Duncan dies.
1959	*The Watch That Ends the Night* (novel; Governor General's Award). Marries Frances Aline Walker.
1960	*Scotchman's Return* (essays). Edits *McGill: The Story of a University*.
1961	*Seven Rivers of Canada* (non-fiction).
1967	*Return of the Sphinx* (novel) and *The Colour of Canada* (non-fiction). Made Companion of the Order of Canada.
1968	Full Professor at McGill.
1971	Death of mother.

1978	*The Other Side of Hugh MacLennan* (selected essays, ed. Elspeth Cameron).
1979	Official retirement from McGill.
1980	*Voices in Time* (novel).
1982	Hugh MacLennan Conference held at University College, University of Toronto.
1984	Royal Bank Award.
1990	Hugh MacLennan dies, 7 November.

The Importance of the Work

Hugh MacLennan's *The Watch That Ends the Night* was first published in 1959. Can the lasting importance of so recent a book be confidently established? Probably not. We can certainly form no useful opinion on the matter until it has been carefully read, absorbed, and evaluated. (If any readers of these words have not yet read the novel for themselves, and are attempting a short cut, I must urge them to set this study aside and acquaint themselves with MacLennan's text. Only then will they be in a position to benefit from what follows.) Nonetheless, it is not unreasonable to begin with the novel's reputation over the years. We often approach a book because it has acquired importance in the opinion of others: we may have heard it recommended by friends whose tastes we share; it may have been set as a prescribed text on an academic course; it may be an acknowledged classic which we feel, in the interests of our cultural education, we ought to read. When *The Watch That Ends the Night* first appeared, it enjoyed a popular success while at the same time earning the respect of literary critics. It appeared for eighteen weeks on the *New York Times* best-seller list, won MacLennan his fifth Governor General's Award, and, with some fairly minor exceptions, received positive reviews in popular and literary journals alike. Since then, it has been read widely, acclaimed by many, criticized by others; a number of literary critics have described it as MacLennan's finest achievement as a novelist. It should therefore be possible to establish the reasons for this response.

Perhaps the main reason may be located in its moving and impressive analysis of the way in which individual human beings get caught up in cataclysmic historical events over which they have no control. This is a quality it shares with *War and Peace* (1865–69), a book which MacLennan studied carefully during the years in which he was writing his own novel. Tolstoy's vast epic-narrative concerns itself with Napoleon's invasion of Russia in 1812, but concentrates on the effects of this campaign on the lives and fortunes of a number of individual Russians from a variety of families. Some are killed in the course of the war; others lose their children or their husbands or their lovers. In various ways, their lives are violently dislocated, and Tolstoy includes many pages of discursive analysis in which he considers why events occurred as they did and who was responsible for them. He concludes that individuals are inevitably overwhelmed by a ruthless process which, once initiated, cannot be controlled or reversed.

It is no coincidence that MacLennan was a great admirer of Tolstoy, that he discussed *War and Peace* in an address, "The Future of the Novel as an Art Form," written while he was at work on *The Watch That Ends the Night*, and described it as "still the greatest novel ever written" (147). There is also a significant reference within the text of *The Watch That Ends the Night* itself (160). I am not suggesting that MacLennan's novel qualifies as a Canadian *War and Peace* — it is a less ambitious, decidedly less assured novel, and it operates at a different level of intensity. But I do suggest that *The Watch That Ends the Night* is the first Canadian novel to deal seriously and compellingly with this crucial and troubling aspect of modern civilization. Since MacLennan's time, other Canadian writers have explored this theme; examples that immediately spring to mind include Rudy Wiebe's *The Blue Mountains of China* (1970), Mavis Gallant's unified collection of short stories, *The Pegnitz Junction* (1973), and Timothy Findley's *The Wars* (1975). But MacLennan was, here and elsewhere, a pioneer so far as Canadian writing was concerned.

Another important aspect of the book is what might be called its spiritual dimension. While it would be misleading to categorize it without any qualification as a religious novel, *The Watch That Ends the Night* is certainly a novel which examines the need for religious — but not sectarian — commitment in human life. (This is not just a matter of belief or disbelief in God; part of MacLennan's subject is the attraction of communism in the 1930s as a materialist political substitute for a lost religious faith.) MacLennan is concerned, then, not with matters of arcane theological dogma but with a pressing psychological need in human beings for belief (to quote a phrase repeated several times in the novel) in "something larger than themselves" (4). In many respects, the novel is a story of a religious consciousness lost but ultimately regained in another form.

This pattern re-enacts MacLennan's own experience while writing the book. As he notes in "Reflections on Two Decades":

> In *The Watch That Ends the Night* my intuitions were forcing me to utter something socially blasphemous in those years. They were asserting that God had not been outmoded by the Christian Church, Bertrand Russell, the social scientists, and modern education.... Not even when I finished the novel had I reached the place where I could say, regardless of whether anyone laughed at me or not, "I believe in God — and that is what scares me." (252)

Clearly this is no easy reversion to a traditional faith, but rather a spiritual awareness attained after much struggle and in the teeth of contemporary trends. For MacLennan, spiritual issues were not matters to be reserved for Sundays and special sacred festivals; he demonstrates how they reveal themselves in all the day-to-day crises of human living. As T.D. MacLulich has commented, "MacLennan's fundamental message in *The Watch That Ends the Night* is that there is no real escape from ultimate issues" (83).

So far, it will be noted, I have been confining myself to matters of content, arguing the importance of the book from the urgent relevance of what it has to say. But *The Watch That Ends the Night* is first and foremost a novel, an order of words that reveals its own unique formal and stylistic qualities. As most critics have observed, it is a fairly traditional novel (some have gone so far as to call it old-fashioned) since it provides the conventional elements of an absorbing plot, intensely human characterization, and a vividly realized setting. On the other hand, it displays certain technical qualities, experimental if hardly spectacular, especially in its manipulation of time. Perhaps its most interesting and original feature as a work of fiction, however, is the way in which it challenges our preconceptions about what a novel should or should not do. In the closing chapters, the didactic element becomes so insistent that, as I shall demonstrate in due time, it threatens to dislocate the narrative structure. For many critics (themselves traditionalist in this respect), this is automatically regarded as an artistic fault. But there can be no doubt, I think, that

MacLennan is making a deliberate (even impassioned) decision here. He is not so much breaking an accepted artistic rule as radically challenging its validity. Some issues are so important, MacLennan suggests, that they take precedence over the tidy preconceptions of literary theory. "The cistern contains; the fountain overflows," wrote the poet William Blake in "The Marriage of Heaven and Hell" (2.58). In this novel, the fountain of MacLennan's urgent vision overflows the containing form of conventional fiction. The book is best read not as timidly traditional but as defiantly at odds with the accepted credos of its time. If there is any validity in this claim, then *The Watch That Ends the Night* (whatever its faults, and few would argue that it is free from blemishes) can certainly qualify as "important."

Critical Reception

At the time of its first publication, *The Watch That Ends the Night* was widely reviewed in newspapers, popular magazines, and learned journals. The response was predominantly favourable, though most of these discussions, inevitably, were brief and relatively superficial. Nonetheless, it will be convenient to begin here with two of the more "academic" reviews that represent the extreme ends of the literary-critical spectrum. Of interest at this point are not so much positive and negative judgements as varying emphases that reflect the varying interests and preconceptions of the reviewers.

Malcolm Ross's review in *Queen's Quarterly* is especially useful for our purpose since it alludes to the range of response in even earlier reviews. The majority of them, Ross observes, concentrated on MacLennan's portrayal of his main characters, with somewhat conflicting results. Others, however, had praised the book for what Ross describes as "curious reasons — as a memorable picture of Montreal, as a perceptive 'political' novel." Ross agrees that these approaches have a certain limited validity, but considers that the prime emphasis should fall elsewhere: "The first (and last) thing to remember about *The Watch* is that it is a religious novel.... [I]ts innermost theme is death and resurrection — and the act of dying into life" (343). Somewhat unexpectedly, Ross goes on to argue that it "is *not* a novel about the 'thirties. Much of the action is *in* the 'thirties — Spain, the Popular Front and all the rest of it. However, the book begins in the present and ends, I suppose, in eternity" (343–44).

This was one of the more probing of the early reviews, and remains valuable for a number of shrewd insights. Personally, I agree with Ross in seeing the book primarily — if not exclusively — as a religious novel; as I have already shown, this is in line with MacLennan's own assessment. But it is only fair to point out that Ross, besides being a pioneering advocate of Canadian literature, was the author of a book on Milton and another entitled *Poetry and Dogma*. These interests would naturally cause him to recognize the religious emphasis of MacLennan's novel — perhaps even to overstress it at the expense of other significant elements. Ross also represents a decidedly traditionalist stance. This is evident in the opening and closing of his review. He begins: "In his latest novel Hugh MacLennan is unashamedly unfashionable. He has something to say!" (343). And he ends: "I would not trade MacLennan for a legion of beatniks or a whole flotilla-full of angry young men" (344). Even at this early stage in the discussion of the novel, we can see the literary-critical battle-lines being formed.

At about the same time, Warren Tallman reviewed the novel in *Canadian Literature* under the curious, seemingly dismissive title "An After-Glance at MacLennan." Tallman was soon to become well-known as a champion of experimental writing, more particularly as mentor to the *Tish* group of poets centred at the University of British Columbia in the early 1960s. He was therefore unlikely to be especially receptive to MacLennan's traditional, even conventional approach to novel writing, and it is hardly surprising that both his evaluation and his emphases were very different from Ross's. Thus he insists that "violence is at the heart of *The Watch That Ends the Night*" (81), and considers Part 5, the account of young Jerome's escape down-river in the canoe, as "up to a level with the very best that has been done in our time" (80). This is an episode, interestingly enough, that Ross never mentions, though it is clearly one of the most memorable sections of the novel and was picked out for praise by a number of reviewers.

But for Tallman, despite its containing "some of the finest writing of our time," *The Watch That Ends the Night* is a "disastrously divided novel" (81). He criticizes MacLennan's lack of any innovative approach to the novel-form, and is especially critical of the presentation of George Stewart as narrator. "Stewart's narrative," he argues, "is badly marred by his mania for handing out crashing complacencies on almost every imaginable major consideration in life: marriage, religion, modern love, art, war, sex, neurosis, politics, philosophy, peace, the seasons" (81). Tallman insists that "what the artist has to tell us is likely to be valuable by virtue of his capacity to represent experience rather than by virtue of any parallel capacity to comment upon it" (81) — a surprisingly traditionalist remark, I would have thought, from someone who might be expected to champion artistic freedom from the constraints of imposed rules. Besides, as Stephen Bonnycastle was later to point out, "Proust, Pasternak, and Thomas Mann are all exceptions" to Tallman's rule (77). I shall, of course, be considering these criticisms in the course of my commentary. Here it is sufficient to notice how two reviewers come to notably different conclusions — in part because of their opposed aesthetic position and assumptions.

If Ross and Tallman represent extremes on a spectrum of reviewing responses, Robertson Davies took a characteristically independent tack in a review for *Saturday Night*. He begins by praising the book in nationalistic terms — "it could not have been written," he maintains, "by anyone but a Canadian" ("MacLennan's Rising Sun'" 119) — but then faces head-on the general problem of MacLennan's didactic impulse and the way in which it can sometimes collide with his artistic ambitions. His earlier books, Davies claims,

> have not always been easy or friendly reading. Always there has been that exploration of his own very Canadian consciousness, which has thrown up boulders of philosophical disquisition on what might have been the smooth lawns of his story-telling. He has refused to bury the rocks and roll the lawns, and has taken the consequences of his decision. (120)

At the same time, Davies believes, against Tallman, that MacLennan has gained "a new mastery" in this novel, and goes on to offer a simple but extremely important insight into the technical aspects of the book. Here, he writes, in a sentence I believe to be crucial, "the story-teller and the self-explorer are one" (120).

Davies does not argue for or against the realistic credibility of MacLennan's main characters, but shows how they are so created that different readers can interpret them in varying but legitimate ways: "It takes a fine novelist, at the top of his form, to create people about whom we can feel, and argue, so strongly" (121). And for good measure, Davies offers his own possibly idiosyncratic interpretation: "My own feeling is that the two men give what is best in life to a woman whom I could not really like; Catherine is a fine example of the spiritual vampire, living on the vital force of others. To other readers she may well seem a true heroine — in Jungian terms, the soul of the hero" (121). Moreover, for Davies, again contradicting Tallman, George Stewart is "the strongest character" in the book, whose "intelligence and insight and worth . . . engage us when we are impatient of the heroics of Martell, and the posturings of Catherine" (121).

Here, once again, we find a reviewer perceptively commenting on the novel while at the same time revealing his own special interests and concerns. Unlike Ross and Tallman, Davies is himself a novelist, and writes with the novelist's interest in psychological motivation, a practical awareness of the techniques of the trade, and a keen ear for reader response. The reference to Carl Jung is not coincidental, since Davies, as his later novels have shown, is himself profoundly indebted to Jungian psychology. He also seems indebted to MacLennan's book. Indeed, not the least interesting aspect of this review is the light it casts on Davies's subsequent novel *Fifth Business*, published over a decade later and notably influenced, so it would seem, by *The Watch That Ends the Night*. This is a point to which I shall return in my conclusion to this study.

We may turn now to the literary criticism and research pertaining to the novel that have accumulated over the years. Since I shall be alluding to many of these commentaries in the course of my own reading of the text, there is no need to consider them in detail here. What needs to be documented and emphasized at this point is the fact that the novel has been the subject of, and shown itself to be responsive to, so many different scholarly approaches. This is not, I would submit, merely a matter of critical ingenuity: it surely presupposes a rich and complex literary text.

MacLennan attracted a remarkable amount of critical attention at the end of the 1960s; no less than four books — by Peter Buitenhuis, Robert H. Cockburn, Alec Lucas, and George Woodcock — appeared within two years. This period coincided with the beginnings of a conspicuous resurgence of interest in Canadian literature, but this interest was itself a by-product of the nationalistic enthusiasm fostered by the centennial celebrations and Expo '67. It is hardly a coincidence, then, that MacLennan's work should have enjoyed a great deal of attention at that time, since he had been the first Canadian novelist to focus his writings firmly upon national issues. Although none of these critical studies was exclusively or even prominently nationalistic in character, all were clearly affected by this aspect of his fiction. Thus Lucas's first chapter is entitled "Constructing a Canada," Woodcock defines MacLennan's main subject as "the fictional delineation of a nation's odyssey" (*Hugh MacLennan* 1), and even Cockburn, whose emphases are more literary than thematic, writes of MacLennan's "voyage into the previously uncharted waters of a nation's spirit and being" (156). But it is Buitenhuis who articulates the point most comprehensively and succinctly:

> In each of his novels, he has tackled a specific area of national concern. In *Barometer Rising* it is the First World War and the emergence of the problem of Canadian national identity; in *Two Solitudes*, it is the French-Canadian problem and the conscription crisis; in *The Precipice* it is Puritanism and Canadian relations with the United States; in *The Watch That Ends the Night* it is the effect of the depression and the rise of fascism on Canada; in *The Return of the Sphinx*, the complex nature of the French-Canadian problem allied to the generation-gap. (19)

These four studies are, of course, introductions to MacLennan's work as a whole, and therefore tend to stress those aspects of *The Watch That Ends the Night* that are most clearly related to his other writings. Buitenhuis's booklet is fairly conventional, but solid and useful. After an initial biographical and general introduction, he proceeds to a book-by-book discussion of the fiction up to *Return of the Sphinx* and ends with a chapter on MacLennan's non-fiction. It is a straightforward, balanced assessment. Cockburn also proceeds book by book, but is decidedly less sympathetic to MacLennan's aims and achievement. He criticizes all the novels for their use of "sociological and historical data" (25), and argues that MacLennan has never succeeded in creating what he himself considered ideal, " 'A whole which is harmonious' " (27, quoting "The Future of the Novel as an Art Form" 147). Cockburn, unlike many commentators, makes no exception so far as *The Watch That Ends the Night* is concerned. For him it is "a disappointing novel" (110); he severely criticizes MacLennan's handling of his three main characters, and argues that he is sometimes "guilty of turgid or slipshod writing" (121). In this analysis, along with Tallman's review and a later article by Francis Zichy, will be found what might be called the main case for the prosecution against the novel.

Woodcock and Lucas open up other, related ways of approaching MacLennan's work, both of which have proved influential. Woodcock lays particular emphasis on "patterns of imagery and symbolism supporting a structure of universal myth" (*Hugh MacLennan* 52), and traces through most of the novels, especially *Barometer Rising* and *The Watch That Ends the Night*, "the Odyssean pattern of journey and return" (89). Lucas discusses each novel under various categories, but it is significant that he pays most attention to *The Watch That Ends the Night* in a generic chapter entitled "Uses of Romance." This is important because, if we approach the book as a romance rather than as a novel in the narrow sense of the term, we shall find ourselves bringing somewhat different criteria to bear. Woodcock's "structure of universal myth" is more easily accepted within a romance than within a novel. In addition, unease about the character of Jerome Martell is less relevant if he is seen not so much as an unlikely larger-than-life figure in a realistic novel but as the traditional hero of romance. This fluctuation between the demands of novel and romance needs to be a continuing concern in any extended interpretation of the book.

Later commentary has tended to be more specific in its focus, though by and large it has refined on one or other of the basic critical positions I have already isolated. In her comparative study of MacLennan and Leonard Cohen, *The Immoral Moralists* (1972), Patricia Morley has provided a historical gloss on Ross's emphasis upon the religious aspect of the book by making a detailed study of MacLennan's Puritan heritage, his *odi-et-amo* relationship with the Calvinism in his blood, and tracing its effects upon his fiction. D.J. Dooley, in a chapter in *Moral Vision in the Canadian Novel* (1979), links Ross's religious emphasis with Woodcock's mythical patterns. The chapter is entitled "MacLennan: Everyman's Escape from the Waste Land," and in it Dooley concentrates on the moral and spiritual ideas that not only underlie the book's didactic aims but also determine its structure. He argues that the book is concerned with "a personal Odyssey" (85) rather than a national one, and also comments, somewhat provocatively, on MacLennan's "daring strategy" in showing "goodness triumphant, not once but three times" (87), a judgement that seems to me arguable but refreshing. T.D. MacLulich, in the most recent of the general studies, his *Hugh MacLennan* in the Twayne series (1983), echoes this concern in his subsection "The

Dynamics of Goodness," but is most notable, in my opinion, for taking up Cockburn's charge and arguing that MacLennan gives George Stewart a "graceful and intimate prose" (79).

Woodcock's focus on mythical structure can be developed in other allegorical readings that lead in various directions. Dorothy Farmiloe harnesses it to a nationalist interpretation by concentrating on the story of Jerome as a child and interpreting it as an imaginative parable of Canadian history. E.D. Blodgett, by contrast, writing in a journal devoted to comparative literature, elaborates on the Odyssean and Oedipal patterns and then follows up references in MacLennan's text to Goethe and Rilke in an effort to relate his work to larger literary and intellectual patterns and contexts.

Politically minded critics have naturally paid special attention to MacLennan's ideology. These include two articles, by S. Lynn and Ann Roberts, in the *Marxist Quarterly* specifically devoted to *The Watch That Ends the Night*, and two more general contributions, by Stanley B. Ryerson and Robin Mathews, to the proceedings of the MacLennan conference in 1982. Such writings generally attack MacLennan's "bourgeois" values and object to his critical presentation of Montreal communist circles in the 1930s. For the most part, they implicitly assume an ideal of social if not of socialist realism and are therefore unprepared to see the novel in terms of anything so potentially escapist as "romance." When such studies judge the book according to party-political rather than artistic criteria, they are rarely of much interest to the literary critic. The most valuable contributions in this area to the study of *The Watch That Ends the Night* are Mathews's demonstration of how MacLennan's political ideology affects the literary structure of his novel, and the Japanese scholar Keiichi Hirano's argument (to be examined in detail later) that Norman Bethune served as a model for Jerome Martell.

In her biography, *Hugh MacLennan: A Writer's Life*, Elspeth Cameron not unexpectedly takes a historical and archival approach. Drawing upon hitherto unpublished letters and manuscripts, she carefully constructs an account of the circumstances surrounding the writing of the novel, its publication, and its reception. I am deeply indebted to this account in one of the sections to follow. In a related article, "Of Cabbages and Kings: The Concept of the Hero in *The Watch That Ends the Night*," Cameron traces MacLennan's attitude to the heroic through the crucial years of the 1950s during which the novel was written, and so throws light on the ways in which the main characters are presented. In 1982 Cameron organized the MacLennan conference at the University of Toronto, to which I contributed a paper which investigated the relation between MacLennan's essays and George Stewart's commenting on things in general within the novel. I tried to show how, by creating a protagonist who was, like MacLennan himself, a public spokesman, MacLennan extended the boundaries of the novel-form to include material usually relegated to "non-fiction."

Perhaps the most impressive and original individual study of the novel, however, is Stephen Bonnycastle's "The Power of *The Watch That Ends the Night*." Bonnycastle is healthily sceptical of the "urge to police the reading of the novel, and impose a single interpretation" (78). He begins from the text itself, and the fact that, although most commentators have found details to criticize in the book, they have generally acknowledged its peculiar "power." He insists that the novel "is essentially about the consciousness of George Stewart and the progress he makes in coming to terms with the world" (80) and makes a simple point which, though earlier stressed in some brief notes by Tom Marshall, is too often ignored: that the larger-than-life, mythic quality which we encounter in the presentation of Jerome and Catherine is not at odds with the realistic aspects of the novel since they are seen through George's eyes and from his perspective. As he remarks: "These characters *are* larger than life to Stewart" (80).

But Bonnycastle is most original (some might say "extreme") in his comparison of MacLennan's achievement here — and, it should be stressed, only here — with such apparently diverse figures as Wordsworth, Proust, and Spinoza. Wordsworth and Proust are both important because of their preoccupation with time and the human capacity to recapture the past through memory, and Bonnycastle, one of the few critics to relate MacLennan's descriptive gifts to the main concerns of his novel, suggests that Wordsworth's record of "Love of Nature Leading to Love to Man," to quote the title of the eighth book of *The Prelude*, is comparable to MacLennan's presentation of George's response to natural beauty that interrelates with his own psychological state. Spinoza is cited because of his emphasis on "Deus sive Natura," or God manifesting Himself within life. Bonnycastle does not claim that MacLennan is the artistic or intellectual equal of these writers, nor does he argue that MacLennan was directly influenced by their work. He is, rather, setting *The Watch That Ends the Night* within a context that distinguishes it from the rest of MacLennan's writings.

There is one slight oddity about this essay. In the early pages, Bonnycastle seems to play down the importance of value-judgements, which he apparently limits to vague discussions of characterization. To be sure, questions such as "Which character do you find most sympathetic?" are generally barren, but value-judgements can, of course, apply to more central matters such as sensitivity to language and control of complex structures. Fortunately, Bonnycastle later acknowledges both the existence and the legitimacy of a "higher" evaluation (80), and is refreshing (and in my view convincing) in his positive response to the conclusion of the novel, where many commentators express reservations. While acknowledging that "critics who dislike [George Stewart] find the ending intolerable" (76), he asserts that the last four pages (i.e., the epilogue) are, for him, "the finest in the novel, because MacLennan reaches a solution to the problem, and a conclusion to his narrative, with a tenderness, a delicacy, and an honesty of which the finest writer would be proud" (82). Readers who share the attitudes and principles of Tallman, Cockburn, and Zichy are unlikely to be convinced. What distinguishes Bonnycastle, however, is his endeavour to read MacLennan not uncritically but at least on his own terms. Bonnycastle is, I believe, the surest guide to what MacLennan intended to convey in the novel. Whether he fully achieved what he set out to do is another matter; different readers will come to different conclusions on this question. But Bonnycastle is alert to the numerous levels on which the novel demands to be read, and many of his insights will be reflected in my own commentary later in this book.

Reading of the Text

APPROACHES TO THE TEXT

"This book is about..."

While George Stewart is a university teacher of history as well as a political broadcaster, his creator was in his later years a university teacher of English as well as a novelist. It so happens that, while a student, the poet-novelist Robert Kroetsch took a course from MacLennan at McGill in 1954 on the history of English prose. He has left us a fascinating account of MacLennan's procedures in the classroom that may be accepted as a model:

> ... I learned the inextricability of style and meaning. MacLennan would seem to start a new book by speaking of its contents. He would begin, simply, "This book is about ..." and end up by teaching us about style. Meaning, for him, inhered, finally, not in what could be said about a book, rather in the complexities and the rhythms and the exactness and the beauty of the prose. It was a lesson in the writing of books; surely a lesson in the reading of his. (138)

I can think of no better way of approaching *The Watch That Ends the Night* than by taking up Kroetsch's hint and following MacLennan's own method.

The Watch That Ends the Night is about — what? One of my teaching-copies of the novel is the fourteenth printing of the Signet/ New American Library paperback reprint (no date given), and the back-cover blurb reads as follows:

Strong, vital, dramatic, stirring... this is a novel that reflects the hungry passions, frantic emotions, and fiery politics of the generation that was young in the thirties. It is the haunting story of two men, one a dynamic and brilliant surgeon, the other a struggling and uncertain teacher — two friends, deeply devoted to each other and deeply in love with the same woman.

That is one version of what this novel is about, though hardly a satisfactory one. Publishers, alas, live in a cut-throat, profits-at-all-costs world and are forced to employ the "hard sell." We are all familiar with that style — it is the style of commercial advertising-copy, of Hollywood publicity, of plot digests in the *TV Guide*, a prose designed to attract viewers to a soap opera. There is nothing in this description that is demonstrably untrue, but MacLennan's novel has been sentimentalized, vulgarized, distorted. The tired clichés ("hungry passions," "frantic emotions"), the simplistic contrast between the two men, the rhetorical repetition ("deeply devoted ... deeply in love"), the standard conventional situation ("in love with the same woman") all conjure up the atmosphere of a Harlequin romance rather than a novel of continuing interest. *The Watch That Ends the Night* may contain all the elements that the blurb-writer exploits, but, if that were really what "this book is about...," I would be wasting my time (as well as that of my readers) in offering this elaborate commentary.

It is impossible to express what this novel is about in a single sentence, but one of the themes that preoccupy MacLennan is the relation, already indicated in my remarks about Tolstoy's *War and Peace*, between private and public worlds and the inevitable struggle between them. This interconnection was impressed upon him early in life — on 6 December 1917, to be precise, when he was a ten-year-old schoolboy in Halifax. On that memorable day, a munitions-ship was involved in a collision with another vessel in Halifax harbour, resulting in the largest man-made explosion before the dropping of the atomic bomb on Hiroshima. Over sixteen hundred people were killed, many more injured, and two and a half square kilometres of the city were totally levelled. MacLennan and his family were fortunate to escape without injury, but the incident left a profound impression upon him. This is most evident in his first novel, *Barometer Rising*, where the explosion becomes the central event in the book and affects the lives and fortunes of all the characters.

But the significance extends much farther than this. The disaster was, after all, an indirect result of the First World War; otherwise, there would have been no reason for a munitions ship to be in the harbour at all. While for most North Americans the war was a remote conflict on another continent, MacLennan knew that its effects could come dangerously close to home — that it was indeed a *world* war. He was therefore conscious at an early age of the continual relation between public events and the private lives of individual men and women. This realization lies not only behind the plot structure of *Barometer Rising*; it dominates *Two Solitudes* and *Return of the Sphinx*, his novels about relations between French and English Canada in the twentieth century, relations whose origins extend back to the Plains of Abraham and the fall of New France in 1759; it is also prominent in his last novel, *Voices in Time* (1980), a novel set in the future after a disastrous nuclear war (a kind of Halifax explosion on a vast scale). In *The Watch That Ends the Night*, world events including the economic depression, the Spanish Civil War, the rise of the Nazis in Germany and the outbreak of the Second World War, have crucial repercussions on the lives of MacLennan's protagonists, but here the interaction of private and public provides more than the main details of theme and plot: it is, in addition, the subject over which the narrator, George Stewart, agonizes throughout the whole book.

This agonizing is, of course, a quality which George shares with his creator. Both belong, in the blurb-maker's phrase, to "the generation that was young in the thirties," or, in MacLennan's own words in a retrospective essay, to "my generation, whose oldest members passed the barrier of childhood amnesia during the First World War" ("Reflections" 247). A child of this epoch, he argues, could hardly avoid the conviction that "a writer should also be a citizen." He admits to being "disturbed by the kind of detachment that enables some writers to rub their hands over the crimes, follies, and misfortunes of mankind because they furnish such exciting materials for literature" (248). MacLennan therefore has absolutely no doubt that a writer should be committed, but commitment has no connection with political partisanship. As he insists in a later article, "The Writer *Engagé*":

> My own notion of the *engagé* has nothing to do with politics in the ordinary sense. I think of a man whose temperament compels

him to involve himself in his time, to live with his antennae naked to the stimuli of his time because he belongs to it. . . . [I]f he is a novelist, he will agree with D.H. Lawrence that the novel "treats the point where the soul meets history." (270)

Here he makes clear that he classifies himself with such writers as Lawrence and Tolstoy and the E.M. Forster of *A Passage to India* rather than with the detached artists like Proust or Joyce.

MacLennan himself made several statements concerning what his novel was about. One, clearly related to the subject of the individual's relation with society and history, described an earlier stage in the evolution of the book but applies well enough to the final version:

My original title for *The Watch* was a dead give-away; it was *Requiem*. Requiem for one I had loved who had died, but also for more: requiem for the idealists of the thirties who had meant so well, tried so hard, and gone so wrong. Requiem also for their courage and a lament for their failure on a world-wide scale. . . .

What *The Watch* was trying to say in the atmosphere of its story was that the decade of the 1950s was the visible proof of my generation's moral and intellectual bankruptcy. ("Reflections" 250–51)

Or, again: "the papier-mâché intellectual armour I had picked up in the thirties contained more built-in obsolescence than any shiny new model you see advertised on the TV screen" (252). It is a devastating charge, all the more so because a kind of wistful sympathy mingles with an almost contemptuous bitterness. MacLennan now realizes that his generation, instead of challenging a discredited capitalist ethic, was in fact "the climax of a philosophy which had been consolidating itself for a century and a half, . . . the materialistic notion that the *quality* of a civilization depends upon its living standards" (252). Such was the philosophy that nurtured the "Silent Generation," represented by Sally Martell and Alan Royce in the novel. This particular comment was written in 1969, a decade after the novel's publication and in the midst of all the challenge and unrest that characterized the late sixties and must have seemed to MacLennan like history sardonically repeating itself.

Small wonder, then, that the writer who had spurned an a-political detachment simultaneously experienced the need to make a separate peace with a frightening and dangerous world. This agonized recreation of the frustrating world of the thirties was also an attempt to transcend the painful realities of history and time. Another of MacLennan's glosses on the novel reads as follows:

> When I began *The Watch That Ends the Night* I was at least clear [that] I was going to write a book which would not depend on character-in-action, but on spirit-in-action. The conflict here, the essential one, was between the human spirit of Everyman and Everyman's human condition. ("Story" 39)

He had discovered that "the basic human conflict was *within* the individual" (39). These two authorial interpretations seem at first sight contradictory, though reconciliation may be possible. Indeed, it might be said that the movement of the novel is from a requiem for the thirties to a painful but liberating realization of the nature of "spirit-in-action." If the first six parts record the former, part 7 and the epilogue may be seen as the proclamation of the latter. It is a gruelling and bewildering journey, a dark journey, but one that has to be accomplished on various levels before one reaches the haven at the end of night.

Novel Versus Romance

"This book is about . . ." leads naturally enough into a related question: what kind of novel is this? The answer to this query, so far as *The Watch That Ends the Night* is concerned, can best be explored by considering MacLennan's professional situation at the beginning of his literary career. He clearly hoped to become both a full-time writer and a serious novelist. Unfortunately, neither the place nor the time, Canada in the early 1940s, was propitious. Nevertheless he made the attempt, and the way in which he tried to satisfy both mass and minority tastes at the same time, whether worked out deliberately or subconsciously, had a palpable effect upon the kind of fiction he wrote. MacLennan was obviously aware that the general reading public favoured a strong story containing plenty of suspense and action, a vividly realized setting, and absorbing human interest.

If he provided these, he seems to have thought, he ought also to be able to include a discussion of serious contemporary issues. As a result, Hugo McPherson has observed, "he adopted the popular romance form and, like Hawthorne, transformed it into an instrument of social analysis and criticism" (700).

His first published novel, *Barometer Rising*, well exemplifies this formula. Neil Macrae, a young man erroneously reported dead in the trenches, returns to Halifax from Europe towards the end of the First World War to clear his name of unfounded allegations of cowardice in action, and to claim the woman he loves. Both attempts succeed, in part through his display of courage and resourcefulness during the Halifax explosion already mentioned. But *Barometer Rising* is more than a story of love and adventure. Neil's antagonist represents the rejected old order of rigid class hierarchy and colonial deference, while Neil himself personifies new attitudes struggling to be born. Close to the surface of the narrative, then, lies an implicit national allegory; the book asks to be read not only as fiction but as contemporary parable.

Moreover, as George Woodcock pointed out in a well-known essay, MacLennan had chosen a plot remarkably close to the archetypal patterns of myth. It should be remembered at this point that MacLennan began as a specialist student in Classics; indeed, he recalls that, as a boy and a young man, he had read comparatively few novels but was steeped in the world of Homeric epic, which seemed to him, while growing up in Nova Scotia, "almost contemporary" ("Midsummer" 13). In other words, his initial conception of story was far closer to the patterns of epic and romance, replete with heroes and heroic action, than it was to the more mundane world of realistic, mimetic fiction. As a result, when he came to turn his attention to the novel as an appropriate means of expression, he naturally introduced strong romance-elements in his plots. Though a number of earlier critics had noted the Promethean and Oedipal characteristics of MacLennan's heroes, it was Woodcock who first pointed out, in "A Nation's Odyssey," an article published in *Canadian Literature*, that Neil Macrae is an early example in his work of the recurrent mythic figure of "Odysseus Ever Returning." The woman he loves is even named Penny — i.e., Penelope. Another Odysseus figure is Archie MacNeil in *Each Man's Son*, a miner turned prize-fighter who returns home unexpectedly to find his wife in the arms of an apparent suitor. The Homeric pattern is altered somewhat, since Archie kills not only the suitor but his (in this case) *un*faithful wife; nonetheless, the basic mythic resemblance remains clear. Yet another modern-day Odysseus is, of course, Jerome Martell returning after having been presumed dead in *The Watch That Ends the Night*, though Jerome resembles Dante's and Tennyson's Odysseus/Ulysses figure rather than Homer's epic-hero in abandoning domesticity for a second journey of adventure and suffering.

Despite the allusion to Penelope and a specific reference to *The Odyssey* on the last page of *Barometer Rising*, MacLennan, in a letter to Woodcock published in a subsequent issue of *Canadian Literature* ("Postscript on Odysseus"), professed to be unaware of this recurring pattern, though he did acknowledge a conscious debt to Tennyson's "Enoch Arden" in the opening of *The Watch That Ends the Night* (see p. 51 below). Be that as it may, the interesting fact that emerges from this discussion is that MacLennan's narratives, for all their clear emphasis on realistic description and acceptable characterization in line with the traditional aesthetic of the conventional novel, contain strong elements of romance. The combination of the two forms allows him, when successful, to tap various levels of significance and so achieve a more universally applicable relevance for his local-based stories. As the critic Paul Goetsch has remarked, "It is the romance, with its air of probability in the midst of improbability, and its proximity to mythic and allegorical forms of order, which enables [MacLennan] to blend catastrophe and affirmation successfully" ("Too Long" 30).

It also allows him to introduce characters of heroic, larger-than-life stature into his fictions, the most prominent — and also, perhaps, the most controversial — being Jerome Martell. I shall be discussing the heroic conception of Jerome in the appropriate place in my reading of the text. Suffice it to state here that Jerome and George are traditional opposites, the former apparently representing the heroic, the active, the adventurous, with the latter personifying the non-heroic, the contemplative, the domestic. I write "apparently" because a complicating factor here is that, ultimately, MacLennan makes a case for George as an alternative hero since the nature of the contemporary world is such that even to survive while retaining one's decency and integrity may be regarded as a heroic achievement. The novel presents, indeed, a modern redefinition of the nature of heroism.

There is, however, another mythic element at work here. If MacLennan is fascinated at the prospect of Odysseus ever returning, he is equally preoccupied, in *Barometer Rising* and in this novel, with characters who return as if from the dead. The Christian pattern is at least as evident as the classical, and there is even a specific reference within the text of *Barometer Rising* to "the resurrection of Neil Macrae" (126). In *The Watch That Ends theNight*, the Christian reference, underlined by frequent biblical allusions, is even more insistent, and it extends beyond the reference to Christian belief and story. I referred at the end of the previous section to this account of spirit-in-action as a dark journey, and the phrase can be applied alike to Jerome's story and to George's. Both of them experience variations of the basic mystical experience in which they must encounter spiritual dryness, the cloud of unknowing, the dark night of the soul — to name different formulations of the same fundamental concept — before attaining an ultimate realization of the Divine.

Readers of the earlier sections of *The Watch That Ends the Night* may well find the above discussion remote from their experience of a story about human relationships in twentieth-century Montreal. But, as the novel proceeds, we come to realize more and more that George Stewart's story is, in a sense, a modern *Pilgrim's Progress*, that MacLennan is gradually leading us from the novel's sanctioned subject of character-in-action to the more exalted concern with spirit-in-action. The challenge of reading *The Watch That Ends the Night* adequately is to adapt to MacLennan's expanding levels of significance. If we are prepared to recognize the romance patterns below the superficially realistic surface of the fictional narrative, we shall be in a better position to combine the multiple but diverse aspects of the novel into a rich and satisfying whole.

"The story of one's story"

MacLennan was certainly a "writer *engagé*" during the composition of this novel. Not only is it a book written in anguish even as it explores the condition of anguish, but it also draws upon circumstances close to his own autobiographical experience. He lived through the various historical periods with which the novel deals, and within his personal life he had also lived through equivalents to some of the more painful scenes depicted here. Although a knowledge of the relations between fictional and real events can make no difference to our ultimate judgement on the value of a work of art, it can help us to understand more fully the creative impulse behind the writing. Henry James once remarked: "There is the story of one's hero, and then, thanks to the intimate connexion of things, the story of one's story itself" (313). In this sense, the story of MacLennan's story is a fascinating one in its own right.

In what follows, it is important to avoid the error of *equating* events in the novelist's own life with fabricated scenes in the novel. George Stewart is not Hugh MacLennan, and Catherine is not MacLennan's first wife, Dorothy Duncan. At the same time, there clearly exists, to repeat James's phrase, an "intimate connexion" between the two pairs. MacLennan seems to have used certain aspects of himself and his wife as basic foundations for his characters, but then transforms them into independent figures, the products of his fictive imagination. Any crude telescoping of fact and fiction on the part of readers is as falsifying as it is reductive, yet to ignore all interrelations between fact and fiction, when the novel in question is as passionately committed to the real world as *The Watch That Ends the Night*, would be equally extreme.

MacLennan showed no hesitation in insisting upon a close connection between the novelist's world and the world of history and personal experience. After all, he had a vision to communicate — one that he considered of vital importance for all his readers — and he therefore wanted what he advocated in his fiction to have an effect upon how they lived their own lives. Any reference to "a fictive universe" or "an autonomous world of art" (favourite phrases of critics who object to a close correlation between art and life) makes no sense in this context. MacLennan was writing about an actual city, Montreal, and described its life and atmosphere at various clearly defined historical periods in the twentieth century. His characters are fictional creations, but they inhabit an existing world, and they live out their fabricated lives in circumstances that are crucially affected by historical movements that possess an actuality outside the fiction. To approach *The Watch That Ends the Night* with a self-conscious artistic detachment is as naïve and inadequate as to assume a simplistic interchangeability between the fiction and the author's biography.

George Stewart, then, is not Hugh MacLennan, but some interesting interconnections can be established between the two. MacLennan moulds his protagonist in such a way that he can incorporate many of his main attitudes and experiences into George's story with the minimum of strain. Thus George, like his creator, encountered difficulties in finding congenial work after graduating in the midst of the economic depression of the 1930s, and so could not turn down a less-than-ideal teaching job at a boys' school. And again like MacLennan himself, George had the opportunity of accompanying a tour to the Soviet Union; consequently, while so many western intellectuals (both within the novel and outside it) were attracted to Russian-style communism at a time when the capitalist economic system seemed on the verge of imminent collapse, he could inspect life under Stalin at first hand and was therefore in a position to compare the myth with the reality. Yet again, he shares his creator's later careers. He is both lecturer (teaching history at McGill when MacLennan was beginning a new career there as a part-time lecturer in English) and commentator (George mainly on radio, MacLennan mainly in magazines).

As I wrote in an earlier discussion of the novel:

By making George Stewart not only a socio-political commentator but the voice through whom the story is told, MacLennan employs a technique by which he is enabled to integrate his own didactic interests into the form and texture of his fiction. . . .

. . . That Stewart, a fictional character, should speak with the same sentiments and in the same accents as Hugh MacLennan, regular essayist in *Maclean's* and the *Montrealer*, is not sad proof of inadequate artistic detachment but a bold refusal to separate imaginative literature from everyday experience. (Keith 57, 59)

But the biographical resemblances extend further. MacLennan's wife Dorothy Duncan, an American by birth who became a writer and even brought the first Governor-General's Award to the MacLennan family, suffered, like Catherine, from a rheumatic heart. She had been told, just as Catherine had been told, that her poor health would never allow her to have children. And here we can see one of the occasions when MacLennan converts the realities of prosaic life into the heightened world of romance fiction. There was no risk-taking Jerome Martell in Duncan's life, and the MacLennans remained childless. At the same time, with some minor discrepancies of dates, the record of Catherine's continually accelerating illness in the novel faithfully reproduces that of his wife. Shortly after Dorothy Duncan's death in 1957, MacLennan wrote an essay-tribute to her under the title of "Victory." There he describes how she suffered an attack of virus pneumonia in 1947 which adversely affected her already damaged heart. "From that moment," he writes, "she was like a city under siege, and the end of the siege was as sure as the last shot in a war. . . . For the last ten years she lived knowing that on any hour of any day she might die" (179).

In an earlier essay, "Christmas without Dickens" (1952), he records how she had to undergo a serious operation late in 1950 during which her life hung in the balance. As Robert H. Cockburn has already pointed out (125), a number of passages from this story are parallelled in the novel. Most notable, perhaps, is a critical moment when, keeping vigil in her hospital room while she lay unconscious, he suddenly "sat upright with the feeling that something had brushed me lightly and passed." He "felt death go out of [the room] and life come back in" (62). In the novel, Jerome tells George at Catherine's bedside: "'Just before you came in, . . . I felt death brush me as it went out of the room" (361–62). MacLennan also allows fiction to follow fact when he has Catherine discover a new creative talent in her last years as she becomes an accomplished painter. Dorothy Duncan had done the same. Indeed, the one painting by Catherine specifically described in *The Watch That Ends the Night*, "a picture of a fourteen year old girl in [on?] a swing lost in a joy of colors that sang like trumpets" (330), is clearly based on one of Duncan's own paintings (a black-and-white reproduction may be found among the collection of photographs preceding the first chapter of Elspeth Cameron's *Hugh MacLennan: A Writer's Life*).

The Watch That Ends the Night concludes just before the inevitable and imminent death of Catherine. Historically, Dorothy Duncan suffered her final embolism on Easter Monday of 1957 and died the following day. For MacLennan it must have been both a harrowing ordeal and a merciful release. The epilogue to the novel presents a moving account of the spiritual and psychological attitude developed at that poignant time. From the final text, it appears obvious that the novel as we know it could not have been achieved until after her death and MacLennan's coming to terms emotionally with the fact of her death. It seems, however, that the novel had a long and complicated gestation. As early as 1950, we gather from a letter, he had been making "sketches for a contemporary novel set in Montreal" (Cameron, *Writer's Life* 252). Oddly enough, these had been interrupted by MacLennan's worries about the progress of the Korean War, the period of political crisis that was ultimately to become the present of the completed novel. Although the last stages of Catherine's illness are apparently based on the earlier stages of Dorothy Duncan's, it is still difficult to envisage what the early plans for the novel could have been like. Until intensive scholarly work has been done on the successive manuscripts and drafts (insofar as they survive), comments must necessarily remain tentative, but it seems clear that from the beginning he was intent on writing a novel aimed, to quote a letter of December 1950, at creating "order out of the general pattern of the life and lives I've seen" (Cameron, *Writer's Life* 259).

Certainly, the novel progressed only slowly through the last years of Duncan's life. We hear of a "breakthrough" late in 1953 and the completion of a preliminary draft by the middle of 1954 (Cameron, *Writer's Life* 273). What his original conception of the novel can have been like remains uncertain, since the version as we now know it seems dependent on a viewpoint that put into perspective the very years of uncertainty, emotional turmoil, and courageous endurance that both MacLennan and his wife were experiencing at that time. An appropriate conclusion to the novel would seem to have been inconceivable in Duncan's lifetime, and it is no surprise that he made little progress with the book in the next three years. Only the death of Dorothy Duncan, and the extraordinary coincidence (if "coincidence" is the right word) of its occurring at Easter, could bring the necessary creative release.

At this point, the story takes a strange turn, which Elspeth Cameron leaves virtually unrecorded in her biography. She is content to make a passing reference to "a dream" (274) and then to quote a long letter to his Canadian publisher in which MacLennan asserts that Duncan "died, in order that this book might be born" and admits to a sense of having been "used by forces very mysterious" (280, 281). But MacLennan went further than this, and in an interview with Roy MacGregor published by *Maclean's* in 1980, recorded an incident that happened just after her death. On the Wednesday following the Easter of 1957, MacGregor reports, with her body waiting to be cremated, he awoke at 4 a.m. in his friend, the poet, F.R. Scott's house, and Dorothy was once again with him. "She was present, very distant," he remembers, his voice shaking. She had a message for him, and it became the guiding force for *The Watch That Ends the Night*, the key to the troubled book he had battled with for years.... (47)

The completion of the novel — in what MacLennan then believed to be its final form — occurred quickly in a burst of writing in the last months of 1957.

But the tortuous saga of *The Watch That Ends the Night* was not yet over. MacLennan sent typescripts to his publishers in Canada and the United States early in 1958. The Canadian publishers were respectful, though they found difficulty in seeing it, in Cameron's words, "as anything other than an autobiographical record" (*Writer's Life* 279). The Americans, however, were dissatisfied with the book because they considered the characters (except Martell) "too trifling as people to be equal to their destiny, especially George Stewart" (MacLennan, qtd. in Cameron 289). Though they were prepared to publish the novel "as a gesture of friendship" (288), MacLennan withdrew it. Ironically, a Canadian publisher's reader criticized Martell as "an inadequate character" (291), so MacLennan must have felt rejected on all sides. Nonetheless, he persevered, made a number of revisions, and the new version not only satisfied Macmillan of Canada but highly impressed Scribner's, who became MacLennan's new publisher in the United States. At the time, however, the publishing history of the book was as troubled and painful as the personal experiences that had given rise to it.

Happily, the actual publication of the novel turned out to be a successful and gratifying event. Reviews were generally positive, and the book sold well in both countries. MacLennan was even able to sell the film rights so, although no film was ever made, it became one of his most profitable undertakings. But his most vivid memory of its publication is told in his essay "New York, New York...." He had been invited down by his new publishers and could hardly believe his eyes when he walked down Fifth Avenue and came to Scribner's window:

> The entire window had been given over to that little novel of mine.... Stacks and stacks of the book were arranged in pat-

terns; in addition there were five large photographs of Montreal, one of Ottawa, and another of a Canadian lumber camp. Blown-up photostats of reviews from the *Times* and the *Herald-Tribune* were in the window. ....
For myself, I stayed there no longer than fifteen seconds, and when I bolted around the corner I was afraid that I had stayed at least ten seconds too long for my safety. The beastie was at my heels. .... (135–36)

MacLennan is being jocular at the expense of his dour Calvinist upbringing, but under the deflating humour we can detect a sense of satisfaction and achievement that was both genuine and well-earned.

Time in the Novel: The Novel in Time

In addition to all the other topics that can complete the phrase "This book is about ... ," *The Watch That Ends the Night* is a novel about time, about its historical fluctuations and the way in which attitudes and assumptions can alter drastically as the years pass. George Woodcock has perceptively described the book as "constructed in receding vistas of time," and has related this structure to MacLennan's "unobtrusively sure" handling of "the leaps of memory" ("Nation's Odyssey" 16). Beginning in 1951, it becomes retrospective to the period T.S. Eliot called "the years of *l'entre deux guerres*" (128). At first, it alternates between present (the 1950s) and past (the 1920s and 1930s), though the pattern is complicated by the well-known "time-loop" in part 5, where we extend backward, in MacLennan's structural and imaginative *tour de force*, to Jerome's pre-First-World-War world. There are, therefore, three distinct time segments in the novel. Or, rather, there *were* three when the novel first appeared in 1959, with the Korean War still fresh in everyone's memory.

But another generation has now passed since then, and for readers of the 1990s, the "present" of the novel has itself receded into the historical past. Indeed, it is with something of a shock that we realize that we are further removed in time from the novel's present than that present was from the world of the Depression and the Spanish Civil War. What was once past and present is now two different stages of the past, and readers who can remember neither stage can never hope to feel the same impact that the novel produced in its own time. We cannot, I think, over-emphasize the extent of this difference. To be sure, all novels change their meaning and relevance in the course of time. Some become hopelessly out of date; others take on a curious new atmosphere unimaginable to the author. A good example of the latter phenomenon is E.M. Forster's *A Passage to India*, published in 1924 when the British Raj was solidly entrenched; it has now become a historical instead of a contemporary novel, though it still retains its power and importance in a world where other instances of imperial domination still operate. If the immediate circumstances have faded, the general application remains unimpaired. *The Watch That Ends the Night* has altered in a somewhat different way. Nowadays, we read MacLennan's account of the university generation of the early 1950s uneasily aware of the era of student unrest that was to unfold little more than a decade later; we also look back from a post-*glasnost* perspective to the most frigid days of the Cold War. The results are eerie.

A notable consequence of this temporal complication is that readings of this novel are likely to differ radically depending upon the age and historical memory of individual readers. Hugh MacLennan himself was born in 1907, and so is to all intents and purposes the same age as George Stewart. He is therefore old enough to have childhood memories of the First World War (most vividly, as I have already noted, of the Halifax explosion of 1917), though he had to rely on research and imagination for some of the details of Jerome's earlier years. Readers who were in their sixties when MacLennan published his novel would have lived through all the historical periods that are portrayed. The young people in the novel itself, Sally Martell and Alan Royce, would probably have at least vague memories of the period of the Second World War, though they would not be able to remember the full force of the Depression. But the majority of people who read the words I am now writing are unlikely to have any memory of the Korean War — or even of the Vietnam war. (I write in the middle of the Iraq-Kuwait crisis, but am still able to assume that a substantial number of my readers will have no memory of any full-scale war, though, by the same token, they live under the shadow of bombs far more devastating than those referred to by MacLennan in his text.)

The response of any reader will, therefore, be considerably affected by his or her time and place of birth. This being so, I must therefore explain my own situation before moving on to my reading of the text. I was born in 1934, so I have no memory of the Depression. But I grew up as a child in southern England during the Second World War, witnessed the Battle of Britain literally raging above my head, and survived numerous air-raids. In addition, I was called up for two years' compulsory military service in the British Army just as the Korean War was drawing to a close. Many of my generation had far closer contact with military action than I did, but it would be folly to assume that my attitudes to a novel that deals with the wars of the twentieth century are not profoundly affected by my personal memories of life under wartime conditions. These will be notably different from MacLennan's on the one hand and from those of current readers of high school or university age on the other. Moreover, while I am roughly of an age with George Stewart's students in the novel, the fact that I grew up in England rather than Canada means that I cannot fully equate my own attitudes with theirs.

Some contemporary literary-critical approaches look askance at this kind of personal commentary, but it seems to me essential as a preliminary when a novel with the historical intricacy of *The Watch That Ends the Night* is being considered. The reading I shall offer in the following pages is obviously affected by my autobiographical circumstances, but I am not claiming that my reading will be in any way superior to those of younger readers — only that it will be different. Allusions that are both obvious and resonant to me (stimulating such reactions as: yes, I remember that!) will inevitably be remote, mysterious, and perhaps dull to others, comprehensible only through recourse to reference books and a conscious effort of the historical imagination. I hope, however, that my discussion will have a certain usefulness as a kind of temporal intermediary between the attitudes of MacLennan himself and those of a generation that came to literary consciousness after the time of the novel's first publication.

INTERPRETING THE TEXT

The Watch That Ends the Night is not a "difficult" book. Its plot is easily followed, and it would seem to raise few technical or linguistic problems. Nonetheless, as I have already shown, critics have disagreed quite forcefully while discussing almost every aspect of the novel. Its characterization has been found convincing by some, superficial by others; its style has provoked both praise and criticism; its culminating vision has been welcomed as profound and dismissed as banal. The following sections contain one reader's commentary. If someone else had been invited to write this book, the resulting evaluation might well have been radically different. There is no ultimate authority on these matters. All I can claim is that I have at least tried to discuss the novel as a work of art rather than as a tract; this means that I place less emphasis on what is said (until the concluding sections) than on how it is said. But — if I may labour a point that ought to be obvious — what follows is offered as *an* interpretation, not *the* interpretation. Readers are invited to test their own responses against mine; if they disagree, and my comments have provoked them to clarify and refine their differing positions, this book will have served its purpose. My aim — the aim of any critic worthy of the name — is to stimulate discussion, to encourage a considered evaluation, but not to impose a judgement.

Title and Dedication

When a novel is told in the first person, the author creates a text which is put into the words of an imaginary narrator-participant. In such instances, the only places where authors can make any clear statement in their own persons are the title, the dedication, and (if included) the epigraph. There is, in fact, no epigraph to *The Watch That Ends the Night*, but both title and dedication merit close attention.

Ironically, MacLennan did not think up the present title for himself. Its original title, he tells us, was "Requiem" ("Reflections" 250), but his American publishers, Scribner's, were unenthusiastic about it, and requested a new one. MacLennan then offered, somewhat halfheartedly, "Sunrise at Evening," and it was this suggestion that inspired a member of the Scribner's editorial staff to propose "The Watch That Ends the Night." MacLennan happily agreed, commenting: "This is the first time I've not titled one of my own books, but I do think it the best of them all" (qtd. in Cameron, *Writer's Life* 295).

"The watch that ends the night" is a quotation from the well-known hymn, "O God, Our Help in Ages Past," by Isaac Watts (1674–1748). The fourth verse reads as follows:

A thousand ages in Thy sight
Are like an evening gone;
Short as the watch that ends the night
Before the rising sun.

This hymn is an adaptation of the ninetieth psalm, a text which is clearly an important influence just below the surface of MacLennan's book. When describing the religious aspects of the novel (two months before the new title was suggested), he wrote to his Canadian publisher:

In the course of writing it I became a religious man, and the book is essentially religious in nature. One night in the Highlands [in the summer of 1958, after he had completed the final revisions to the novel] its real theme came to me. It is contained in the [third] verse of the 90th Psalm: "Thou turnest man to destruction; and sayest, Return, ye children of men." (qtd. in Cameron, *Writer's Life* 286)

But this is no ex-post-facto rationalization. Reference is made to this psalm — and, indeed, to this verse — in the text of the novel: Catherine quotes it to George on the day following the Montreal demonstration, just before Jerome leaves for Spain (253).

When a writer places considerable emphasis on an earlier text, it is often helpful to examine the immediate context as well as the lines actually quoted. The ninetieth psalm, traditionally attributed to Moses, concerns itself with God as an eternal and omnipotent force, and with the ignorance and powerlessness of human beings who exist under His sway. It contains seventeen verses in all. I quote here (from the Authorized Version) those that seem to me especially relevant to *The Watch That Ends the Night*:

1 Lord, thou hast been our dwelling place in all generations.

2 Before the mountains were brought forth, or ever thou hadst formed the earth and the world, even from everlasting to everlasting, thou art God.

3   Thou turnest man to destruction; and sayest, Return, ye children of men.
4   For a thousand years in thy sight are but as yesterday when it is past, and as a watch in the night.
5   Thou carriest them away as with a flood; they are as a sleep: in the morning they are like grass which groweth up.
6   In the morning it flourisheth, and groweth up; in the evening it is cut down, and withereth.
7   For we are consumed by thine anger, and by thy wrath are we troubled.

. . . .

10 The days of our years are threescore years and ten; and if by reason of strength they be fourscore years, yet is their strength labour and sorrow; for it is soon cut off, and we fly away.
11 Who knoweth the power of thine anger? even according to thy fear, so is thy wrath.
12 So teach us to number our days, that we may apply our hearts unto wisdom.

When he came to adapt the psalm for his hymn, Isaac Watts altered the tone. From its first line onwards, "O God Our Help in Ages Past" is less dour. Reference is made to "the stormy blast," but God is seen as "Our shelter from the stormy blast." An unspecified "watch in the night" becomes "the watch that *ends* the night," with an interpolated reference to "the rising sun." The relation between God's wrath (or, more disturbing, His indifference) and God as a source of "help," "hope," and "shelter" becomes one of the dominant concerns of MacLennan's novel. The uncertainty of human life — especially Catherine's awareness of how "it is soon cut off" — is another.

The implications of the title are, in fact, teasingly ambiguous. The "watches" of the night were ancient divisions (three or four in Jewish usage) inaugurated by vulnerable peoples who had to be perpetually on guard against nocturnal attack; more recently, the term applies to military (especially nautical) guard duty. The watch that ends the night presumably anticipates a welcome dawn, but also draws attention by contrast to the dangers of the night; it may even contain a hint of a last period of rest before a dawn battle. William C. James lists the "watches" in the narrative as "the afternoon that Jerome spends watching over Catherine's unconscious form" (327), George's extended wait before his union with Catherine, and the long years of Jerome's absence. It can also refer, on a mystical level, to the closing stages during the progress of the dark night of the soul; or, if one sees life in this world as a vale of tears (the slogan of the MacLennan clan was "The Ridge of Tears" [Cameron, *Writer's Life* 5]), it can even suggest a period of waiting and suffering before a final release. This is, I assume, what E.D. Blodgett means when he writes: "The final title has the value of declaring one of the central themes of the novel as transience of life . . ." (282). We may remember that the title of his first novel, *Barometer Rising*, presides oddly over a novel dominated by the disastrous Halifax explosion; in MacLennan, joy and sorrow, optimism and pessimism, are always intermixed.

If the title draws attention to some of the major themes in the novel, the dedication provides a hint of the deeply personal urgency that lies behind the book. *"Tibi, ubicumque sis aut qualiscumque, gratiae et hic liber."* The Latin is straightforward, but difficult to translate satisfactorily into clear flowing English. A reasonably accurate, albeit somewhat awkward, translation is: "To you, wherever and in whatever form or condition you may be, thanks and this book." The "you" (in the original Latin, the second-person singular is closer to the French "tu" or the now antiquated "thou") refers, of course, to Dorothy Duncan. I say "of course," but in fact this is a connection only available to those who are aware of the circumstances of MacLennan's first marriage. For most readers who encountered the book at the time of its first publication, the dedication was mysterious. When I first read the novel, for example, I knew nothing of the background, though my instinct told me that there must have been a deeply personal dimension to the book. For the small percentage of those original readers who noticed the dedication, and who were in a position to translate it, however, it confirmed a specific autobiographical connection between the art and the life, even if the details of that connection were not yet available. MacLennan is drawing public attention to the intensely personal experience out of which the novel springs.

Part 1: Voices from the Past

"There are some stories into which the reader should be led gently, and I think this may be one of them." A one-sentence opening paragraph as simple and spare as any that can be imagined: twenty-one words, the longest of which is composed of no more than seven letters. There is only one word, "led," which contains even the faintest hint of metaphor. Ernest Hemingway himself couldn't have been more direct or apparently unliterary. At the same time, this is an interesting opening: we are gripped by the indirect implication that there are depths to be plummed, uncertainties to be approached gingerly, shocks to be sustained. Above all, there is a sense of personal urgency communicated here — an urgency that never relaxes throughout the story. Without revealing anything about the kind of story he is telling, the narrator has immediately created interest and suspense. We are, in modern parlance, "hooked": we want to read on. This is the simplicity of a master story-teller.

In the next paragraph, we are given much of the essential information that we expect early in a novel that conforms to a predominantly realistic mode. The setting is Montreal, the month February, and the year "the first winter of the Korean War" (3). If we consult an encyclopedia, we learn that North Korea invaded South Korea in June 1950, so the first scene — indeed, the whole of the novel that is not retrospective — takes place in 1951. But why are we not told this directly? The answer to this question, which cannot be given with any confidence until we have read further in the book, is of considerable interest.

The Korean War was in its time the most serious threat to world peace since the end of the Second World War in 1945. It became a crucial test of the strength and effectiveness of the United Nations, whose forces eventually repulsed the invading army and preserved South Korea as an independent nation-state. All this may seem remote history half a century later, but its significance to people of MacLennan's — and his narrator George Stewart's — generation can hardly be exaggerated. The United Nations' predecessor had been the League of Nations, founded in 1919 after the First World War, an organization that had signally failed to prevent armed conflict in the 1930s, whether in China or Spain or in the full-scale fighting of 1939–45 — the very wars in which Jerome became involved in the retrospective portions of *The Watch That Ends the Night*. Moreover, the Korean War, like the Spanish Civil War, involved communist and non-communist forces (though the ideological background, especially of the non-communists, was very different in the two cases). In referring to "the first winter of the Korean War" rather than simply to "1950–51," MacLennan is alerting us to the historical and political emphasis that is to play so important a part in the subsequent narrative.

Another reason for the indirection occurs in the next two paragraphs, during which the narrator introduces himself and tells us something of his life and work. We already know that he teaches at a university (readily identified by anyone with even minimal background knowledge as McGill), but we now learn that he is also a broadcaster and journalist commenting on current political issues. Again, he insists that he is "a product not only of Montreal but also of the depression, scarred by it like so many of my friends" (3). This gives us some indication of his age (we later discover, more precisely, that he is "forty-four" [93]), and of his historically determined attitudes.

In these early paragraphs, we can also deduce a good deal about the narrator's character. Even his name may be meaningful. He introduces himself as "George Stewart," and in a conference paper I once suggested that there might be something significant in the fact that this name "combines the surname of the aristocratic 'good old cause' with the Christian name of the first of the bourgeois Hanoverians" (Keith 59). David Staines, as commentator on the session, cast doubt on this suggestion (68), but I still think that it has some merit. The Stuarts of the eighteenth century (both spellings occur in the original records, and it is worth remembering that George has just delivered "a pleasant and at times witty lecture on the witty and at times pleasant eighteenth century" [15]) represented in the popular imagination a world of romantic glamour — Bonnie Prince Charlie, and all that. The Hanoverians, whose dynasty began with four Georges, were the first British constitutional monarchs, and generally abrogated the romance of kingship (George III rejoiced in the nickname "Farmer George"). Here, George Stewart is "just old George" and "Comfortable old George" (20, 39) to his stepdaughter. In a novel in which the qualities of heroic action and passive survival ("I felt like a survivor," George comments a little later [6]), the romantic and the commonplace-domestic, are split between Jerome Martell and the narrator, who is attracted to the heroic but cannot attain it himself (at least in its traditional manifestations), a name that combined these same contrary associations is not, surely, inappropriate.

George makes clear from the start that his desires are modest, and centred upon an unspectacular but contented home life: "I was looking forward to the walk home along Sherbrooke Street, ... then to a drink before my fire, to dinner and after dinner to a quiet evening with my wife, a little more work and a good night's sleep. That evening I was happy" (3). These anticipations may seem unpretentious, even humdrum, but we soon realize, as we proceed through his retrospective account of the 1930s, that such modest wants constitute a privilege. "That evening I was happy." On the opening page of a novel, we are probably justified in interpreting this as a danger signal (in the first act of a tragedy, it might even suggest *hubris*). Again, the words are as simple as possible, yet their implications are manifold. Two pages or so later, the question "Must one remember or is it better to forget?" (5) conceals similar complexities. The query is subtly positioned. Little does George know that in a few minutes he will be forced to remember the past in searing detail, will realize painfully that forgetting is no longer an option.

The directness of the opening two or three pages is achieved by an almost studied avoidance of image and metaphor. We eventually find, however, that MacLennan gains a notable effect by deliberately confining the imagery in George's narrative to a limited number of cumulatively impressive references. Perhaps the first prominent example of metaphorical speech occurs when he writes of his wife, "I had made Catherine the rock of my life" (6). The image immediately suggests a solid protection in a world of instability, and is therefore appropriate to George's representative story of enduring in a frighteningly unstable world. But the specific metaphor is one that gathers around itself numerous biblical associations. In the Jewish scriptures, the Old Testament of the Christian Bible, God is continually referred to as "the Rock" or "my rock" (see, for example, Deut. 32. 4, Sam. 22. 2, Ps. 18. 31). And most readers will recall the punning words of Jesus about the disciple Peter (whose name means "rock," as is clear from its French equivalent "Pierre"): "upon this rock I will build my church" (Matt. 16. 18). The relevance of these passages to George's remark is profound. God, they imply, is the only sure foundation; Jesus had to entrust his Church to a fallible human being, and there is a sad irony in the fact that he chose Peter, the first (temporarily) to deny him. By the end of *The Watch That Ends the Night*, George will have learned that, however admirable a person Catherine may have been, to regard another human being as a rock is inevitably a mistake.

I lay emphasis on this allusion, however, for a further reason. As we proceed through the novel, we shall notice that George's narrative is studded with phrases that hark back to the Bible or the Prayer Book. Here are some instances:

> She had loved Jerome with all her heart and with all her soul and with all her mind. (34; cf. Mark 12.30)

> So that summer I entered Arcadia and the pipes played and the glory of the Lord shone round about. (60; cf. Luke 2.9)

> [The Martells] believed, they believed at last, that goodness and mercy would follow them all the days of their lives.... (214; cf. Ps. 23.6)

> Silence, and after a while I murmured the line about one generation passing away, another coming and the earth remaining. (263; cf. Eccles. 1.4)

The list could easily be extended. The point that needs to be made here is that George Stewart is typical of his generation in that his language is steeped in the imagery and rhythms of the Bible. Although in the same paragraph in which he describes Catherine as the "rock of [his] life," he declares, "In the Thirties I had said to myself: There is no God," and later, "What difference does it make if there is no God? Or, if God exists, why worry if He is indifferent to justice?" (6), the cultural influence of Christian beliefs and attitudes is still with him. In other words, a Christian cultural tradition is present within the very language he uses. Furthermore, since the novel is one in which some kind of religious faith — however tentative, however qualified — is ultimately regained (see the extended quotation of Jesus's words about the kingdom of heaven on the final page [Matt. 25.14–21]), the continuity of biblical reference is an important novelistic effect.

When George goes on to describe Catherine's rheumatic heart and the effect of her physical condition upon both their lives, he employs another common image while observing that "she must live with the sword dangling over her head every minute of every day" (6). The reference, of course, is to the sword of Damocles, a phrase everyone understands though few remember the occasion in classical history that gave rise to it. This allusion provides another illustration of MacLennan's palpable but ostentatious art. The image remains latent in our minds for most of the book until it is used on three occasions in the twelfth chapter of part 6 (322, 324). And at this point, reference is also made to the world of the 1950s "prosperous under the bomb" (323), and we come to realize how the story of the sword of Damocles applies to us all, and how Catherine's situation is, at one level of meaning, an emblem of the contemporary human condition. The point is made explicit in the concluding chapter of the novel: "The sword was still over her as the bomb was over the world" (371). Although MacLennan's metaphorical usages are numerically few, they are employed carefully and creatively, and we shall do well to pay attention to them.

Such is the effect created in the opening pages. We are presented with a domestic, thoughtful, middle-class narrator who has survived the tumults of the first half of the twentieth century, and appears to have entered a period of relative calm. But the ever-present threat of his wife's frail health continues, and a sense of impending crisis intrudes into the narrative. Suddenly an unexpected sword-stroke falls. Four simple words over the telephone represent a voice from the past that is immediately recognized as a threat within the present. Into what has seemed a life-pattern of almost dull ordinariness comes an event so strange as to be virtually unthinkable: a man George "had thought dead for a decade" (8) re-enters his life. Moreover, we gradually realize that Catherine had once been married to this resurrected man. The plot thickens. I use this hackneyed phrase, redolent of old-fashioned melodrama, because it appropriately sums up Mac-Lennan's surely intended effect. A book which started in the mode of drab realism suddenly shifts to contain an extreme situation suggesting the symbolic mode of myth or archetype; or, in the terminology already explored, realism has become shot through with the pattern of romance.

It is, in fact, an age-old device. As many reviewers recognized on the occasion of the book's first publication, MacLennan is presenting a twentieth-century version of the story told by Alfred Tennyson in his once-popular Victorian narrative poem "Enoch Arden." Tennyson's poem begins with three children, two boys and a girl, who have been playmates in an English seaside village. Both boys fall in love with the girl, who eventually marries one of them, Enoch Arden, a sailor later believed to have been lost at sea. After she then marries her second childhood sweetheart, Enoch returns, but, discovering what has happened, leaves without revealing himself to the married pair. The basic plot recurs in various folklores and cultures, but, as one Tennyson commentator has written, "The poem's absorption into common life is reflected by the fact that 'Enoch Arden' is now a generic term used to refer to any man who leaves, is presumed dead, and returns to find his wife married to someone else" (Marshall, *Tennyson Handbook* 146). MacLennan here fuses this traditional story pattern with that of his favourite Odysseus theme to create the romance foundation for his story of love, the demands of political involvement, and the quest for spiritual value.

MacLennan opens his novel, then, with great care and in so doing displays considerable artistic skill. The second chapter, recording the conversation between George and Jerome, moves quickly and crisply, and need not detain us. In the third chapter, George phones Catherine, then meets Sally and her boyfriend Alan Royce. All this is straightforward enough until we encounter a curious conversation between George and the college porter in which the latter comments on the anomaly between the twenty-below Montreal winter and the fact that "the glaciers are melting" (18). There seems no necessity for such an exchange, but the passage is important for its atmospheric and even cosmic associations. Imagery of melting, moreover, recurs throughout the book. George employs it, for example, towards the end of the chapter when he observes how winter reminds him of his youth "and of the time before the glaciers began to melt" (23). It turns out to be an equivocal image that can suggest either emotional release or potentially threatening and uncontrollable change, yet another of the evocative image patterns that hold the novel together.

The recurring image of "cold" is hardly surprising in a novel set in a Montreal February. It is to be noted, however, that politically 1951 and the Korean crisis set the book firmly within the period of the so-called Cold War. Especially at that time, the word had political as well as climatic connotations. On the other hand, the related image of "melting" connects with the emotional temperature of the story. George, reiterating his love for Catherine, calls her a "rock" once again, but adds: "When she smiled like a little girl I melted" (26). Later that evening, in a scene of domestic affection, he holds out his hands to her "and she rose as I tugged and melted against me" (28). From these instances, we can see quite clearly how imagery interlinks what might otherwise seem disparate elements within the whole.

Another image which occurs for the first time here, and becomes one of the most compelling in the book, is that of explosion. The references in part 1 are minor, though the first echoes in an interlocking fashion the passage I have just quoted. Of Catherine and her difficulties with Jerome he remarks: "No wonder Jerome had exploded against her" (33). The second, more characteristically, is political: George expresses his confidence that the Korean War "would not blow up into the big one everyone feared" (38). The word, carrying over from the Halifax explosion as portrayed in *Barometer Rising* and foreshadowing the nuclear disaster in *Voices in Time*, anticipates the violence so prominent in all MacLennan's fiction, whether expressed in military, political, or sexual terms. If we include its cognates and synonyms, it occurs well over twenty times in the course of *The Watch That Ends the Night*, and, as might be expected, it is most often associated with the turbulent character of Jerome.

So far I have tried to show how, in the opening of part 1, MacLennan admirably lays the foundations upon which the main structure of his novel can be built. There is, however, one aspect of this section still to be discussed where, at least in this reader's opinion, he is less successful. I am referring to his portrayal of the younger generation as represented by Sally and Alan Royce. Since *The Watch That Ends the Night* is, as we have seen, a novel about time, and since the main time scales of the novel concern the 1930s and the 1950s, it is important that the generation of the latter be well represented. Yet MacLennan's main characters all belong to the former, and, given George Stewart's first-person perspective, a fair representation of younger people is rendered all the more difficult.

The problem, however, is one not so much of sympathy as of understanding. George is disillusioned by his own generation, and claims to prefer the younger. "Was there ever a crowd like ours?" he asks. "Was there ever a time when so many people tried, so pathetically, to feel responsible for all mankind?" The young, he argues, seem to him more mature "because they know nothing of the 1930s." He sees them as "so much freer in their souls than we had ever been, and so much easier in their emotions." He sees them, moreover, as graduating into an easier, more fortunate world, with a greater sense of stability and security. "They all expected to get jobs and marry young and to raise families young, and now as I walked down the corridor I felt joy flood me as I heard the happy noise they made at the end of their day" (4). There is surely a touch of sentimentality here, and I have to say that I remain unconvinced by the whole line of argument. Sally, the most prominent representative of this generation in the novel, is twenty-two. She was therefore sixteen, just coming into adult consciousness, at the beginning of the nuclear age. To be sure, her generation missed the desperation of the Depression, and was too young and too far away to comprehend the full significance of the Hitler years. But hers was the generation that witnessed the revelations of the Holocaust and saw itself as inheriting the moral burden of the atomic bomb. I cannot believe in that "happy noise at the end of their day" as an adequate representation of a general attitude.

Like many novelists, MacLennan is, I believe, uncertain when presenting characters younger than his own generation. (Similar problems arise in *Return of the Sphinx* and, to a lesser extent, in *Voices in Time*, both of which contain scenes set in the 1960s.) Alan Royce, with his deliberately artificial, consciously pompous, polite but semi-parodic responses to George, is acceptable enough as a lightly etched minor character, but Sally, the assured biology major with supposedly enlightened psychological attitudes, is a different case. George assumes a playful irony (" 'Freud and you little girls' " [23]), but he seems to admire her no-nonsense confidence, which comes across as too easy a contrast to the insecurity he sees as characteristic of his own generation. The scene in which they discuss deeply personal matters while walking through a frozen Montreal (images of the waste land conspicuous in the background) is ambitiously conceived but less successfully rendered. The conversation opens as follows:

"You're exceptionally taciturn tonight," Sally told me.
"Considering what you think of my talking too much, nothing could please me more than to hear you say that." (18)

This strikes me as false, even if one grants that both are uneasy about raising intimate and possibly embarrassing matters. The dialogue is stiff and unconvincing compared with the telephone conversation between George and Jerome in the previous chapter. Thematically significant statements are made — Sally's verdict on Hemingway and the attitudes his novels embody; the questions "Who am I? Whence come I?" (22), questions which Sally shares with George here and later in the novel (though earlier in time) with Jerome — but the conversation as conversation is hardy dazzling.

The remaining chapters in part 1 are reasonably straightforward. Not only are we introduced to Catherine but we come to know more about George's attitude towards her and their mutual dependence upon each other. Other key words in the novel, especially "mystery," "spirit," and "fate" (25–26) are introduced. The telephone call from Harry Blackwell, parallelling Jerome's, represents another voice from the past and makes us realize that the past is inevitably to be relived. The revelation of Jerome's return to Catherine is simply and movingly presented, and George's sense of politicians losing control of politics in a world that "seemed to be falling apart" (37) clearly establishes a link between his personal situation and that of the world in which he lives. Sally's compulsion to speak about her love for Alan, neatly in terms of plot if unconvincingly in terms of credibility — " 'What was Mummy like when she was my age?' " (49) — nudges George into the recalling of his own years of growth and love, that "strange time" (46). These scenes represent MacLennan the careful and experienced craftsman rather than MacLennan the probing and original thinker-novelist. Nonetheless, the storyteller's spell is still potent: our interest has been firmly caught and we want to read on.

Part 2: The Ignominy of Boyhood

In part 2, we move back to a simpler world before the Depression or the Second World War, and, more specifically, to the world of George's and Catherine's childhood. George is seventeen years old (which means that it is 1923 or thereabouts), and he has just returned from a canoe trip with some of his school friends in northern Ontario. At a first reading, this detail seems insignificant, but we realize later that it sparks off a direct contrast with Jerome Martell:

whereas George was on vacation when exploring the wilderness (itself emblematic of an earlier Canadian past), for Jerome it represented a harsh world from which he desperately escaped at the risk of his life.

In the opening pages, however, it is Catherine who is seen as in danger of her life. For all the seeming peace of a Westmount August, this is "the years of *l'entre deux guerres*," but the society involved looks back to the past rather than forward to the future. George's father (symbolically christened Hastings) can only recreate the battles of the past — a pastime which is seen as itself dangerous. He is introduced as "leaning on a cross bow of his own manufacture which was certainly as lethal as any used at Agincourt" (54), and Catherine has almost been killed by walking into the archery butt at the wrong time. Hastings Stewart is the first of the comic-grotesque characters in the novel who seem almost Dickensian in their vivid oddity. (Dr. Bigbee of Waterloo School is the most memorable.) If *The Watch That Ends the Night* were no more than a conventional realistic novel, such figures would be rightly criticized as overdrawn caricature, but MacLennan is using them, as Dickens did, to underline the thematic concerns of his book. George's father lives only in the past, in a child's world of stylized violence where (at least in theory) nobody gets hurt. A living symbol of what a preoccupation with history ought not to be, he is shown a little later with the local children "playing the battle of Jutland" (73). From him, George clearly inherits his fascination for history, but fortunately the son recognizes the past not as an escape from the present but as the force that moulded and perhaps even determined the present.

George is originally led into his remembrance of things past by thinking of the first time that he really saw Catherine, when she was "dressed in green" (50). In consequence, part 2 finds him back in the green world of pastoral. By the beginning of the second chapter, he is quite explicit about this: "So that summer I entered Arcadia and the pipes played..." (60). Traditionally, the pastoral world appears a pleasant place (here we have moved significantly from a frozen February to the heat of August); it is not, however, a world exempt from death, as the constant laments for dead shepherds in pastoral elegies and Nicholas Poussin's two great paintings entitled "Et in Arcadia Ego" ("I am also in Arcadia") indicate. Catherine escapes the recreated perils of Agincourt, but her "poor little heart" (55) and her recurrent sickness are emphasized from the start. "Arcadia" is here a delicate, "innocent," and miraculous time of young love, but harsher forces are forever threatening to overwhelm it. These include not only Catherine's precarious health but also worldly reality in the form of George's witch-like Aunt Agnes, another Dickensian figure — symbol rather than caricature — in the presence of whom George and his father almost blend into Pip and Joe Gargery of *Great Expectations* when confronted by Mrs. Joe or Miss Havisham. We realize that this fragile house and the green world that contains it are constantly at the mercy of outside forces that ultimately control them. Such forces cannot be ignored or defied. Significantly, the father is ruined financially by the one speculation in which he acts without consulting Aunt Agnes. The resultant fall into poverty foreshadows on a personal level the effects of the Depression on a far greater scale a decade later.

But this pastoral world is primarily a world of romance, and the main subject of this section becomes the mutual but frustrated early love between George and Catherine. At this point we encounter a controversy that invariably arises when MacLennan's fiction is discussed: his capacity to present scenes of sexual intimacy. The standard position — amounting to something close to a consensus — is that MacLennan, despite the anti-puritanical attitudes in most of his writings, is himself puritanical when sexual matters are involved. As early as 1951, George Woodcock complained of "a suave mawkishness in talking about sex which amounts almost to diplomatic evasion" ("Nation's Odyssey" 17). Robert H. Cockburn wrote in similar terms: "as is always the case with MacLennan vs. Sex the particulars are decorously skirted" (113). T.D. MacLulich, writing specifically of this novel, observed that George "occasionally affirms the existence of his sexual desire, but we are not quite sure we should believe him" (87). Alec Lucas is the one non-conformist in this critical chorus. On the subject of illicit sex in MacLennan he writes, "such intimacies are generally vague but not prissy" (23), and observes generally: "For the modern reader, accustomed to an almost clinical discussion of every form of sexual behaviour and misbehaviour, MacLennan's standpoint may seem timid or even dishonest. Yet the love scenes are neither" (24).

While it would be foolish to deny a certain staidness and unease on the presentation of sex on MacLennan's part, an attitude that was characteristic of his generation, I incline, so far as this novel is concerned, to Lucas's position. A number of complicated factors are involved here, including the historical circumstances under which the novel appeared. It is worth remembering that *The Watch That Ends the Night* was published several months before the well-known New York district court decision to remove the Post Office ban on the circulation of the unexpurgated edition of D.H. Lawrence's *Lady Chatterley's Lover*, a decision that effectively heralded in the so-called "age of permissiveness" so far as the literary presentation of explicitly sexual scenes was concerned. This decision was handed down on 21 July 1959.

In Canada, a similar case was originally heard in the spring of 1960 in the Quebec Superior Court, where MacLennan himself, along with Morley Callaghan, testified in defence of Lawrence's novel. At that judicial level, the judge ruled that *Lady Chatterley's Lover* was indeed an obscene book, and the case passed through the Court of Queen's Bench and the Supreme Court of Canada (with the poet-lawyer F.R. Scott acting as a defence counsel) before the latter court finally voted five to four against the banning of Lawrence's novel on 16 March 1962. Meanwhile, the famous "trial of Lady Chatterley," Regina versus Penguin Books Ltd., at London's Old Bailey, had come to a similar decision by a jury verdict on 3 November 1960. (For a useful account of these matters, see Djwa 340–48.)

MacLennan was writing *The Watch That Ends the Night*, then, in a context sensitive to various legal as well as social constraints. He had something important to say about the nature of human life, and wanted to reach as wide an audience as possible; he clearly had no wish to stir up controversial matters that might divert attention from his main concerns. Besides, in an article she wrote about her husband in 1945, Dorothy Duncan had remarked that he could never understand "the embarrassment of the older generation over what they chose to term his use of 'too much sex'" (39). Similar sentiments persisted into the late 1950s. MacLennan's treatment of sexual subjects may seem tame today but in his own time it was considered extreme.

Another historical point needs to be stressed. Sexual mores — at least within middle-class North America — underwent an extraordinary change during the 1960s. In fact, this change was so extreme that it is difficult for young people of the present day to understand the accepted "rules" on such matters that existed in the earlier period. It is even more difficult for contemporary novelists to portray scenes that take place in the earlier age without seeming stiff or stuffy — "prissy," in Lucas's phrase. The problem, therefore, is not MacLennan's alone. As it happens, Hugh Hood wrote frankly and impressively about this very subject in *A New Athens* (1977), a novel set in the period during which MacLennan was writing *The Watch That Ends the Night*. His protagonist, Matt Goderich, is recounting a scene not unlike that between George and Catherine:

> Her body was pushed right up against mine. I considered sliding my hands around tentatively, then decided not to. I did not want anything that might spoil her bright sweet goodness. How abstract that sounds! I'll express it in the terms of today. I didn't want to sleep with her because I thought it might damage her feelings about herself, and about me, and I didn't want to act promiscuously. (77)

Hood is writing on this side of the permissive divide, but is trying to reproduce, as faithfully as possible, the feelings and moral code of the previous age. He is only too aware that his commentary may seem "stuffy," but he feels bound to establish the difference in attitude. The following passage is, I believe, crucial in the way it illuminates our response to MacLennan's novel:

> Our sexual feelings and attitudes have been so modified between 1952 and 1966 that the earlier date seems an eon removed from the way we live now....
> I can say exactly what I felt and thought about Valerie. I knew that she was wonderfully pretty and attractive. I loved kissing her, holding her, and I loved the excitement she stirred in me — ready, achieved sexual potency. But I didn't want to make physical love to her — mere, bare intercourse. That might have ruined something. I make no apology for this belief. We were very young. We were experimenting, finding out by cheerful and honest play, with many subtle mutual agreements shared almost openly, what the sexual merry-go-round was like, what it was for. (77)

MacLennan belongs to a generation earlier than Hood's; indeed, Hood's Matt Goderich is almost exactly the age of Sally in MacLennan's novel. I consider Hood's account to represent a far surer communication of his generation than MacLennan's, for the reasons given in my discussion of part 1. But in describing George and Catherine in 1923, MacLennan is on his own ground. His characters are even younger than Hood's Matt and Valerie, and the scene he describes constitutes an equivalent rendition — equally true to its particular period — of "the sexual merry-go-round."

In presenting this scene, MacLennan is not attempting to present what Cockburn calls the "particulars" of sex. Instead, he is recording the uneasy first steps in a perilous adult relationship on the part of two young people in the 1920s attempting to balance sexual instincts against romantic idealism. I have entitled this section "The Ignominy of Boyhood" because W.B. Yeats's words from "A Dialogue of Self and Soul" (written in the 1920s) brilliantly recapture the frustrations and fumblings of that uneasy period of maturation. Yeats writes of

> that toil of growing up;
> The ignominy of boyhood; the distress
> Of boyhood changing into man;
> The unfinished man and his pain
> Brought face to face with his own clumsiness. (2. 1887)

This surely sums up George's attitude perfectly.

If we judge from this viewpoint, there is a touching poignancy about this relationship. The young George is both embarrassed and afraid. Inevitably, it is an account of sexual failure. The climactic scene beautifully conveys this sense of adolescent awkwardness. Catherine, significantly, is the dominating figure; while George is still at the stage of hand-holding, he feels Catherine's "will, her woman's will, taking possession of [his] weaker male one" (78). In this novel, with the singular exception of Jerome Martell, the women are consistently stronger than the men: Catherine and George, her parents, his parents, Norah and Harry Blackwell, Jerome's foster parents — even, until he is provoked into murder by her sarcasm, Jerome's mother and the engineer. In Catherine's case, this is exacerbated by her knowledge that her time may be running out. Her desperate need for sexual experience represents a stage that George has not yet reached, either physically or emotionally: "But I trembled and was afraid not merely as a boy is who fears to make a girl pregnant, but because I was not yet a man" (78–79).

The delicacy here, the tentative expression of sexual uncertainty, is George's, and wholly appropriate to the situation. Intimate physical details would be grotesquely out of place; they are part of what George fears and so cannot bring himself to consider. MacLennan is not fudging a sex-scene here but poignantly communicating an experience of failure that will have considerable repercussions in terms of George's psychology and also of the pattern of his subsequent life. Indeed, the scene may be regarded as a crucial test in any response to MacLennan's art. At first, he seems to be writing a conventional tale of young love; but the expected pattern doesn't materialize. He follows neither the traditional convention (assertions of love with the physical details decorously banished off-stage) nor the more modern predilection for point-by-point explicitness. George is caught between romantic notions of love and the conflicting imperatives of sexual reality. His recollection of the scene is itself triggered by Sally's no-nonsense, almost clinically scientific attitude to sex, love, and marriage. We shall not appreciate the full complexity of this scene until we realize that historical determinants, awareness of how behavioural norms change in the course of time, a sense of individual and social duty — all the themes, in fact, that are central to *The Watch That Ends the Night* as a whole — are factors that unite, ironically and pathetically, in this presentation of a failed union.

Part 3: Casualties

With the exception of the Epilogue, part 3 is the shortest section of the novel, containing only two chapters. Nothing essential happens, and it would be easy to conclude that it represents no more than a bridge passage between more significant recollections. Further consideration, however, reveals the fact that each chapter focuses on a minor but thematically significant figure within the book. Both are recognized as casualties. The word is used twice of Connolly, the CBC man who prepared George's broadcasts. First of all, he has been "a genuine hero and casualty" of the Second World War (86), during which he had been decorated for bravery in the Air Force. "Hero and casualty" is a striking combination. It recalls what we have already learned of Jerome Martell, though both words have rather different connotations when applied to him. This is an inconspicuous but typical instance of MacLennan's structural art; Connolly's function within the novel is minimal so far as the plot is concerned, but he is instrumental in helping us to place, by means of comparison and contrast, the attitudes and status of the major characters.

More to the point, however, we are told that Connolly was "more seriously a casualty of Ernest Hemingway," having been so steeped in the American novelist's writings that his own attempt at a novel read only "like a parody of the later Hemingway parodying the Hemingway of the Twenties" (86). We have, of course, already encountered Hemingway in part 1, where Sally made her critical remark about those " 'appalling adolescent he-men like Hemingway and all those naive idealists thinking they were so terrific because they went to bed with each other to prove the capitalist system stank' " (20). Because Hemingway was such a key literary figure during the decades portrayed in *The Watch That Ends the Night*, he attains a kind of emblematic significance within the narrative. A veteran of the First World War who served as a war correspondent in both the Spanish Civil War and the Second World War, he wrote novels and stories that condemned warfare and its traumatic psychological effects, yet also created a special kind of hero who made a separate peace in the course of saying "a farewell to arms" but combined this with a taste for toughness and violent action. MacLennan, who admired him as stylist and artist but came to deplore his values, clearly introduces him (and Connolly) to highlight his own more equivocal analysis of heroism that begins by centring on the related though ultimately very different figure of Jerome but ultimately focuses, as we shall see, on the apparently unheroic figure of George himself.

In the total scheme of the novel, then, Connolly (who never appears again or is as much as mentioned after this chapter) acts as little more than a foil. On the one hand, he represents the more belligerent extreme of reactions to the Cold War, a right-wing position that contrasts dramatically with Jerome's left-wing sympathies; on the other, in his bull-headed militancy he throws George's considered political analysis into impressive bold relief. MacLennan does not, however, limit himself to effects of crude contrast. When, after insulting George and storming out of his office, Connolly returns to apologize and admits, " 'I feel inferior' " (89), we recognize a link (perhaps explained by the shared experience of their generation) with

George. We remember George's own self-assessments: "I have never felt safe. . . . I have never seemed mature to myself" (3, 4); "I had never had any confidence in myself" (77). If Connolly is a "casualty," perhaps George is also.

Balancing Connolly in the succeeding chapter, however, is the more prominent and ultimately more disturbing figure of Arthur Lazenby. Lazenby is the third voice from the past to have broken upon George in less than twenty-four hours, "another of those figures who would always be associated in [his] mind with the depression" (88). The two agree to meet for lunch in Ottawa after George's interview with the Minister of External Affairs (who, incidentally, in "real life" at this time was Lester B. Pearson). The immediate reason for their meeting is Lazenby's pressing need to weigh the political implications of Jerome's reappearance. Although now a highly placed civil servant, we learn that he was once a card-carrying member of the Communist Party and obviously fears, in the critical days of the Korean War, potentially embarrassing revelations. Through George's shrewd assessment, MacLennan portrays him in terms that, once again, are broadly etched and close to caricature: "He talked suavely of politics for fifteen minutes, dropping just the right number of names in just the right way, and if there was any civil service cliché I had ever heard, he did not miss it" (95).

Once again we detect a mask erected in an attempt to shut out an awkward past. Casualties. If the word applies to both Connolly and Lazenby, it can also be applied, as we have seen, to George — and, by extension, to Jerome and Catherine. "There but for the grace of God, I thought, went something," George muses as Lazenby disappears, and his connection with this particular casualty becomes all too evident: "And what a generation I belonged to, where so many of the successful ones, after trying desperately to hitch their wagons to some great belief, ended up believing in nothing but their own cleverness" (101). The time is ripe, clearly, for a reassessment of that generation, a painful recalling of the period so many wished to forget. This need has been initiated, so far as George is concerned, by the return of Jerome, and coincidentally by Sally's continuing curiosity about her father, and now a third recognition is added. Casually glancing out of the window as his train back to Montreal stops at a small station, George recognizes someone he knows: a French-Canadian still working as porter at Waterloo School where George had taught during the depression years. Coincidence? Perhaps, but this further jolt to the process of memory is consonant with the interlocking determinants of MacLennan's art. George has escaped from his servitude at Waterloo; Ti-Jean Laframboise had not. "[T]here but for the grace of God," he thinks, echoing his earlier thought, "might I be still" (102). The scattered, half-suppressed recollections begin to come together: George's unavoidable confrontation with his painful remembrance of things past is clearly at hand.

Part 4: Threatening Shadows

It is at this point that George Stewart becomes recognizable not just as a moderately interesting individual but, implicitly if not explicitly, as a representative Everyman figure as well. Here his experiences become typical of a generation. As he notes in the second paragraph, "three things happened to me, as they happened to millions of other young men at that time. I lost my faith in religion; I lost my faith in myself; I lost my faith in the integrity of human society" (107). Similarly, when he protests at his father's failure to come to terms with the present, he admits to indulging in "the kind of talk young men used in the depression" (108).

The Great Depression, of course, haunts this book as it haunts so many of the novels of mid-twentieth-century North America. Unregulated and often irresponsible commercial expansion and financial speculation in the 1920s resulted in the disastrous Wall Street crash of October 1929, which led inexorably to numerous bankruptcies and staggeringly high unemployment figures that continued through most of the 1930s. The effects of all this coincided with bad harvests on the prairies and the sufferings of the so-called "dust-bowl years" vividly portrayed in Canadian fiction in works like Sinclair Ross's *As for Me and My House* and, more obliquely, Margaret Laurence's *A Bird in the House*. Although Quebec and Ontario in fact suffered less than other parts of the country, the industrial poor were hard hit by lay offs and a sharp decline in the number of available jobs. Social welfare and relief systems were both rudimentary and inadequate. These conditions are themselves only hinted at in *The Watch That Ends the Night*, but their psychological impact explains the emotional temperature which MacLennan catches so well, and which lies behind the political arguments and actions that disrupt the life of Jerome Martell.

Because of the effects of the Great Depression were experienced by a high percentage of the Canadian population, its memory is deeply ingrained in the popular consciousness. The political events in other parts of the world, notably in Europe, between the end of the First World War in 1918 and the beginning of the Second in 1939 are more hazily retained in public memory. But these, too, are essential background to the action of the novel as recurrent references to events in Germany, Austria, Abyssinia, and Spain make clear. It may therefore be helpful to outline the main historical developments here, since MacLennan assumes some general acquaintance with the main details of the volatile international political scene.

The European situation at this time stems ultimately from the large-scale effects of the defeat of Germany in 1918 and the harsh conditions imposed upon the country, in terms of the return of disputed areas to neighbouring countries and economically crippling financial reparations, at the Treaty of Versailles in the following year. These duly led to catastrophic inflation, the collapse of the German currency, and a vast national bitterness which soon manifested itself in the founding of extreme political parties, including Adolf Hitler's National Socialists or Nazis. The re-established German republic tottered uncertainly through the 1920s, but in 1932 the Nazis made notable gains in the elections, and Hitler was appointed chancellor early in 1933. In the same year, after winning a substantial parliamentary majority, he was invested with over-riding political and military power, and the infamous Third Reich was proclaimed. On the death of Hindenburg, the president of Germany, in 1934, Hitler assumed the title of Führer and quickly established an efficient but ruthless totalitarian police-state. Meanwhile, Benito Mussolini had formed a Fascist party in Italy and come to political power as early as 1922. Late in 1934, he used a border incident involving Italian-dominated Eritrea and Abyssinia (Ethiopia) as an excuse for attacking the latter country, and completed occupation within two years. At about the same time, the Christian Socialist chancellor of Austria, Engelbert Dollfuss, set up a dictatorship on the Fascist pattern and attacked the socialist strongholds in Vienna. But his apparent military success led to his downfall; he was assassinated by Nazi extremists in 1934 and his country was absorbed into Hitler's Germany by 1938.

But it was the situation in Spain that caused the most conspicuous and vigorous concern among intellectuals in the 1930s. For many years the country had been split between Monarchist and Republican rivalries. In an election in 1931, though the Monarchists returned a majority, the Republicans scored heavily with urban voters, and King Alfonso XIII left the country, though without abdicating, on the demands of the Madrid Revolutionary Committee. Bitter conflicts between extreme political parties, Communist and Fascist, continued in the early 1930s, a situation complicated by deep-rooted pro-clerical and anti-clerical sentiments. In July 1936, an army mutiny in Spanish Morocco led by General Franco quickly spread to the mainland, and the clash between the Communist-dominated Popular Front (or Loyalists) and the Fascist Nationalists led not merely to civil war but to international intervention on both sides. Hitler and Mussolini both leant their support to Franco, while Stalin initially aided the Loyalists, though he abandoned them when they had served his own political purposes, when their strength faltered and they became, in Jerome's words in the novel, "nothing but an embarrassment" (296). Jerome is presented as leaving Montreal for Spain in the spring of 1937, when ideological commitment was at its height. By the time he briefly returned to Canada late in 1938, he was well aware that the cause was lost, as he makes clear to Lazenby (296–97). Within a few months, Franco's Nationalist forces had triumphed.

By this time, Hitler's Third Reich was firmly embarked on its ruthless program of territorial expansion. In 1936 he had defied the League of Nations and the rest of Europe by reoccupying the demilitarized zone of the Rhineland, a necessary act for the establishment of efficient military and industrial power. Then, using the demands of the Sudetenland area of Czechoslovakia as a convenient excuse, he threatened the integrity of the whole country, creating a crisis that led to the notorious Munich Pact of September 1938, where the British Prime Minister Neville Chamberlain was instrumental in maintaining a fragile peace by the sacrifice of Czech independence. Despite assurances of "peace in our time" this resulted, with the assistance of Poland and Hungary, in the absorption of most of Czechoslovakia by the spring of 1939. Shortly thereafter, Hitler turned his attention to Poland. It was the invasion of Polish territory, following the even more notorious non-aggression pact with Stalin, a callous agreement between Fascist and Communist dictatorships, that led to the outbreak of the Second World War in September 1939.

Against this sordid world-political scenario, George Stewart makes his first tentative steps towards an independent and mature life. But MacLennan doesn't make the mistake of presenting the early depression years as a long and relentless chronicle of deprivation. George shared the difficulties of finding employment with countless others, but the circumstances under which he eventually obtained work were bizarrely unique. The account of his years spent teaching at Waterloo School represents the high point of MacLennan's Dickensian streak. A graduate in history meets his Waterloo indeed when he finds himself teaching anything but history in an English-language school in Quebec, once "the house of a prosperous French-Canadian landowner" (110), that boasts the motto *"Caveat Gallus"* ("Let the French beware"). The corridor "where the stuffed heads of lions, tigers, impallas [sic], rhinos and African buffalo stared at each other like family portraits in an English country house" (110) clearly parodies a form of British imperialist mentality. As D.J. Dooley notes, Waterloo School "is a smaller and more confined garrison outpost than Montreal" (82). The eccentric headmaster, Dr. Lionel Bigbee, who is presented as "entirely surrounded by stuffed birds" (111), also surrounds himself with a teaching staff of English flotsam and jetsam (George, sent from an educational employment agency by mistake, is, in a phrase that speaks volumes, "the first native" [114]) and maintains his outpost of empire grotesquely unaware that history has long passed it by.

Fantastic as all this may seem, MacLennan was here drawing upon his own experience. As Elspeth Cameron's biography indicates, apart from setting Waterloo further out in the Quebec countryside instead of in a suburb of Montreal, MacLennan modelled his fictional school on Lower Canada College, where he had himself taught between 1935 and 1945. Bigbee is a fictionalized version of the headmaster of that time, C.S. Fosbery, who lived in Canada only during the school year, returning to England by the first boat at the beginning of the summer holidays. From Fosbery, MacLennan borrowed Bigbee's physical description, his voice, his manner in the classroom, and his amazing energy that gave the impression of his running the whole of the school single-handed (see *Writer's Life* 101–04). The whole Waterloo School interlude provides a sardonic commentary on the outdated attitudes that were partly responsible for the economic and political conditions of the time, yet it also serves as an allegory of Canadian historical development. By the early 1950s, we are told, the school is Canadian-run: the portraits of British admirals have been replaced by those of Canadian prime ministers, and it has made remarkable gains in efficiency, though George is honest enough to acknowledge that it had also lost something of its zany idiosyncrasy (118). Nonetheless, while the episode, like the vignettes of George's father, offers comic relief from the harsh realities of the real world, it is shocking to realize the slightness of MacLennan's caricature.

Set against this lightly etched, impressionistic satiric comedy is MacLennan's equally impressionistic but movingly immediate portrait of Montreal at this period. The city is presented in many moods, but never more memorably than in George's vivid account of the social conditions he witnessed on his free weekends:

> Never before was Montreal as it was in the Thirties and it will never be like that again. The unemployed used to flow in two rivers along St. Catherine Street, and I used to see eddies of them stopping in front of shop windows to stare at the goods they could not buy. There was a restaurant that used to roast chickens in its window over electrically-operated spits, and there were always slavering men outside staring at the crumbling skin of the chickens and the sputtering fat. I remember how silent the unemployed were when they emerged after a snowfall to clean the streets, often without mittens on their hands, and how pitiful their cheap worn shoes looked as the snow wet them and turned the unpolished leather gray. And above all do I remember my own guilt as I saw them, for I had work and they had none. (119)

Some commentators have criticized MacLennan for giving an incomplete portrait of Montreal at this period. Stanley B. Ryerson, though he alludes obliquely to this passage, has even gone so far as to claim that the unemployed "are barely present" in the novel (15). But this is to misunderstand — and fail to respond to — MacLennan's art. *The Watch That Ends the Night* is not a novel about the unemployed in the thirties, but, since social issues were so central to the place and the age, they are conspicuously present. The paragraph I have just quoted may not loom quantitatively large in relation to the rest of the book, but qualitatively it makes a deep impression. Indeed, it haunts the novel, and I would be prepared to argue that it constitutes the most prominent single image in the whole book. Imaginatively, MacLennan catches both the atmosphere and the conscience of the age in that image of the poor slavering in front of the restaurant window or that of the mittenless hands and the discoloured shoes. A similar image occurs a few lines later when George recalls "the hideous olive-green street cars of that period with their graying conductors half-sitting, half-standing in their cages at the back while the crowds read the bad news in the papers" (119). This is, surely, a fictional equivalent of T.S. Eliot's crowds drifting over London Bridge in *The Waste Land* and has a similar imaginative impact.

Here we need to remember Bonnycastle's insistence that the whole of *The Watch That Ends the Night* is filtered through the viewpoint of George Stewart. This is *his* Montreal. It is irrelevant to point out, as Jacques Brazeau does, that the novel "n'ajoute rien à la connaissance d'une agglomération montréalaise francophone" (44; [adds nothing to our knowledge of a Francophone Montreal community]). The author of *Two Solitudes* is here presenting the city from the viewpoint of one of the solitudes. Novelists are under no obligation to present the whole of the society in which they set their novels. There are many Montreals, and we can go elsewhere for excellent, different (and equally incomplete) contemporary portraits — to Mordecai Richler's *The Apprenticeship of Duddy Kravitz* for working-class Jewish Montreal or Gabrielle Roy's *Bonheur d'occasion (The Tin Flute)* for the viewpoint of the French-Canadian poor.

George Stewart's perspective is unabashedly middle-class. The point is emphasized at various points in the novel. His artist friend Adam Blore is the most assertive: " 'You know, George, you're that very rare thing, a perfect specimen. You're middle class to the bone. You're a nice guy. All you want is a nice little wife and a nice little apartment and a nice little job . . .' " (132). The assessment is a combination of the kindly, the critical, and the condescending. George himself significantly rephrases it a little later: "Adam Blore was right when he called me a bourgeois at heart. What else is a bourgeois but a man who wants a home, some respect from his fellows and a feeling that he has a future and belongs to a human group?" (157). Such figures have rarely been popular as literary protagonists; the very word "bourgeois," in general usage, implies a placing sneer. MacLennan, in a curious way, is being original, challenging, even perhaps revolutionary, in daring to suggest that an unostentatious, timid, socially and politically uncertain figure like George Stewart is worthy of serious attention. He is even bold enough to suggest that the George Stewarts of this world are at least as worthy of respect as the Jerome Martells.

The pattern of this section may now be becoming more clear. After ten years away from home, George returns to find everything the same yet not the same. His father is still living in the past (his latest invention is an improved crossbow) while Waterloo School symbolizes the dead hand of a moribund history. His fellow teachers are a portrait-gallery of the outmoded and the dispossessed; Shatwell, for example, the most prominent of them in the narrative, "had failed in teak in Calcutta, in jute in Madras and in rubber in Kuala Lumpur" (117). Through Adam Blore (an eccentric who had significantly been expelled from George's respectable school) he is introduced to a more contemporary Montreal, "a group of angry and discontented young people who met to drink beer, make assignations with each other and talk about politics and art" (120). They offer him, if (and MacLennan surely invites this) we are prepared to interpret the section in allegorical or at least representative terms, the temptations of political commitment (Norah Blackwell urges him to become a member of the Communist Party) or a plague-on-both-your-houses Bohemianism. Significantly, it is within this context that George obtains news about Catherine and hears intriguing stories about her doctor-husband.

Earlier in the novel, George remarks to Sally about Alan Royce: " 'You're giving this boy a terrific build-up' " (19). It soon becomes apparent here that MacLennan is giving Jerome a terrific build-up. First, Caroline Hall describes him as "the most attractive male animal in Montreal" (121). The iconoclast Adam Blore then calls him "dumb" and "dangerous," classifies him as "a primitive," "an idealist," and "a stallion," but also acknowledges that he has "five times more energy than any normal man" (132). When George sees him for the first time, he considers him "shorter than I had imagined" but "burlier" and "much older than I fancied myself to be." "Physically ruthless," he nonetheless possesses "a rueful smile that was completely charming" (136). But descriptions are weak compared with the impression we receive from Jerome in person. "Why the devil didn't you marry her when you had the chance?" he asks within seconds of meeting George (138), and in the next chapter we see him in action demolishing the theoretical socialist from *The New Statesman* (another of MacLennan's Dickensian caricatures of representative types). "Never in my life," George observes, "had I seen a man who had this singular capacity to set a room on fire" (146).

By the opening of the final chapter of part 4, we might be forgiven as readers for believing that the centre of attention had turned from George to Jerome. First, Catherine tells George about Jerome's lightning wooing, a scene that reveals him as the extreme opposite of the timid George. Then, at the Martells' summer cottage in the Laurentians, a setting that leads smoothly and appropriately into the wilderness-landscape of the ensuing section, Jerome initiates the process of recollection that is going to reveal the curious circumstances of his own past. Here sex and violence are tellingly intermingled. In a shamed reaction after having contracted a sexual disease, Jerome seeks death on the battlefield. In the process he kills eleven men with a bayonet, an act which in itself sounds like part of the traditional myth of heroic action but is presented as a confession of guilt and horror ("the bayonet is murder" [166]). And this leads to a crucial comment on his war-decoration: "'I was given the M.M. [Military Medal]. For committing murder because I'd caught the clap, I was called a hero" (167).

Is he or is he not a hero? Most dictionaries distinguish at least three different meanings for the word: "a man of distinguished valour"; "one invested with heroic qualities in the opinion of others"; "the principal male character in a story." Hitherto, we have accepted George as "the principal male character" of the story, but Jerome is now seen as a candidate for "hero" in the first two senses of the word. MacLennan plays skilfully with the possible ambiguities here. To Sally at the beginning of the novel, Jerome is anything but heroic. Jerome himself looks upon the official recognition as grotesque. Our modern literary instincts cause us to regard the term with suspicion if not embarrassment. George himself is an example of "the principal male character" who manifests anything but the traditional heroic qualities. Yet MacLennan, as we have seen, was brought up as a student of heroic literature and had been drawn to the romance-form which still finds a place for "the hero." Moreover, he has now introduced a figure into the narrative, however ambiguous, who seems to exemplify the character of the old-style hero. As Jerome, the potential hero, announces, "I don't know who I am" (169), and prepares to explain why, the stage is set for a new perspective on the heroic and its place in the modern world.

Part 5: Dark Journey

Part 5, recounting Jerome's escape down the river as a small boy, is generally regarded as a high point in the novel and as one of the most memorable scenes in all of MacLennan's fiction. MacLennan himself saw it as such, and even Warren Tallman, perhaps his harshest critic, praises the section for its "traumatic intensity of perception" which lifts "the representation up to a level with the very best that has been done in our time" (80). It is certainly a bold stroke from the technical point of view. Whereas hitherto the odd-numbered parts have taken place in the novel's present of 1951, and the even-numbered ones have returned to George Stewart's earlier life in the 1920s and 1930s, the pattern is broken here as we take a further time-journey back into an earlier past. Moreover, the centre of attention shifts from George to Jerome, and, although much of the narrative is recounted in indirect speech through George as mediator, a number of paragraphs reproduce Jerome's own words.

The narrative itself, with its sense of terrifying sexual violence presented from the viewpoint of a young boy who cannot comprehend the full implications of what he sees and hears, is vivid in its nightmarish intensity. But this climax gives way to the suspense of the boy's perilous escape from the dangers of the lumber-camp and the gripping account of his canoe-journey downriver. In a novel that is set for the most part in the bustling streets and crowded conditions of a modern city, the contrast created by this solitary journey through wilderness is extreme indeed. There is no need, I think, for any detailed discussion of the literal narrative at this point. What demand attention, however, are the various other-than-literal ways in which the scene can be interpreted.

Jerome, as I have already established, is a character presented in heroic as well as realistic terms. At one level, this account of Jerome's active and traumatic childhood is clearly offered as a notable contrast to George's pastoral account of his own youthful years. We are invited to shift our ways of reading quite radically at this point. In the previous section, we have seen Martell as a vigorous, charismatic, politically committed Montreal surgeon within a novel that offers a historically faithful portrait of the city in the first half of the twentieth century. But his almost spectral presence in part 1, as a man who has returned as if from the dead, should have alerted us to other generic possibilities. We now begin to see clearly that Jerome is not merely being offered as the principal male figure in a story but more exactly as the traditional hero of a romance.

As is well known, one of the distinguishing features of a traditional hero is his mysterious origin. The most famous instance within the western tradition is, I suppose, the story of Moses in the bulrushes as recounted in the second chapter of Exodus. This pattern of the hero as foundling is frequently repeated in works of literature where the hero needs to be provided with an unusual origin. In Henry Fielding's novel *Tom Jones* (1749), for example, the comic hero who, as his name indicates, is presented as the most ordinary of human beings — plain Tom Jones — is nonetheless given the hero's tell-tale mysterious birth: he is comically deposited as a small baby in the bed of the local village squire. Similarly, in Thomas Carlyle's philosophical extravaganza *Sartor Resartus* (1833–34), the central figure with the heavily symbolic name of Herr Diogenes Teufelsdröckh is left in a cradle on the doorstep of a poor family in a small community. These somewhat bizarre instances from modern literature are clearly displaced forms deriving from mythic archetypes. Besides Moses, we may remember how Oedipus, in classical legend, was ordered by his father to be exposed on a mountainside but was secretly brought up by a remote herdsman. A similar story is presented by Shakespeare in his dramatic romance *A Winter's Tale*, where Perdita survives an analogous adventure. Even the story of Jesus, with its account of miraculous origin (the immaculate conception) and escape from premature death (the slaughter of the innocents and the flight into Egypt) can be recognized as a sublime religious version of the same basic pattern. MacLennan's Jerome, who does not know his father or his surname or even where he was born, fits clearly into this recurrent *topos*.

Reference to the story of Oedipus, however, also raises the possibility that MacLennan's story can be interpreted in psychological terms. We know from Elspeth Cameron's biography that MacLennan "had begun reading Freud's work in earnest about 1930" (78). Clearly, he had no more than an intelligent layman's understanding of modern psychological theory, but it is equally clear that the patterns of his writing are influenced by his reading of Freud and the popular Freudianism that was typical of his generation. In *Each Man's Son*, the young Alan MacNeil witnesses the murder of his mother by his father when the latter returns (after the pattern of Odysseus) to find her in the arms of a suitor. Here Jerome is in the next room and hears the sounds of love-making and the quarrel that results in the murder of his mother by the engineer. This variant on Freud's "primal scene" and the oedipal rivalry between child and father (or father surrogate) obviously invites psychological interpretation. Moreover, the whole relationship of George and Catherine is fraught with psychological complexity. If it is true, as many critics have claimed, that George, whose own father is so ineffective, adopts Jerome as his surrogate father, then his eventual marriage to Catherine after Jerome's supposed death contains deep psychological significance.

We can also look at this section of the novel from a more historical viewpoint, with special emphasis on the development of Canadian awareness and a Canadian tradition. From this perspective, Jerome's journey represents a foreshortened version of another basic pattern: from wilderness to city, from the lumber-camps that were so important in the economy of eastern Canada at the turn of the eighteenth and nineteenth centuries to the strategically important position of the seaport of Halifax in the early twentieth century. The MacLennan who had himself been born in an isolated community in Cape Breton and had moved outwards, first to Halifax and then to Oxford, Princeton, and Montreal, was in an excellent position to portray a figure who embodied this national development.

If we read this section with the possibility of a historical interpretation in mind, we shall see how careful MacLennan has been to document a historical progression. In the first paragraph, he emphasizes "primeval forest" (173). In the second, he conjures up the past of "a century and a half ago when the Royal Navy harvested this forest for masts" (173). Jerome even asserts that he had once seen a man flogged. The intention, surely, is to represent Jerome's personal past as an image of the country's development through history. In her article "Hugh MacLennan and the Canadian Myth," Dorothy Farmiloe has explored this aspect of *The Watch That Ends the Night* in the greatest detail. Jerome, she argues, "symbolizes the Voyageur"; he possesses "the same survival tactics that enabled the early coureurs de bois to exist in the wilderness" (146). She points out how the setting for this section, authentic as it may be, is also allegorically appropriate for a historical reading: "Jerome Martell's story is a re-enactment springing out of the symbols peculiar to Canadian history — the canoe, the river, the immense wilderness — embodied in a powerful and exciting narrative that emerges as a pure Canadian classic" (149).

It is, of course, possible to take this kind of interpretation to extremes. When Farmiloe remarks that Jerome "escapes in his canoe (the voyageur's only means of transportation), the engineer (society) following him in the motorboat" (147), I can appreciate the force of the argument while at the same time resisting the rigidity of such a reading. To her credit, Farmiloe immediately draws attention to the danger herself: "To continue categorizing in this manner, however, is to risk turning a very fine tale into a one-for-one allegory when it suggests so much more" (147). For my part, I would not wish to go so far as to see Jerome exemplifying "not only the search for the Canadian identity but the split personality caused by the two cultures in our national consciousness" (147). Nonetheless, I cannot help acknowledging that this is the kind of larger significance that MacLennan's novels continually evoke. His didacticism inevitably encourages extrapolation beyond the immediate terms of the narrative. However, any serious literature invites thought that expands beyond its own boundaries, and I think that Farmiloe is right to argue that Jerome's river-journey in this section "is a Canadian counterpart to Huck Finn's flight down the Mississippi on the raft and ought to occupy the same place in Canadian literature that Huck's holds in American" (149), though Jerome is, as Tom Marshall has stressed, "a primitive seeking civilization, Huck Finn in reverse" (15).

Moreover, the historical relevance of this section extends beyond the canoe-journey itself. Jerome's voyage ends at a small river-town, identified by Robert H. Cockburn, himself a Maritimer, as Newcastle (116), where he encounters industrial society in the form of the railway; MacLennan encourages such a reading by his reference to Jerome's "entrance into the organized world" (195), where he takes part in that early North American labouring practice of "hopping trains" (197) or riding the rods. On arriving at Moncton, he is befriended and subsequently adopted by the Martells, who represent the tradition of Protestant Christianity. They teach him how to pray

(213-14) and bring him up in a faith that emphasizes duty, service, and unworldliness. But the world interferes relentlessly, and Jerome's pastoral upbringing in Halifax, roughly equivalent to George's Arcadia in Montreal, is shattered by his traumatic experiences in the First World War, where he encounters sex and violence once again on a large scale and is robbed of the simple faith he had derived from his foster parents. This loss of innocence also has national implications (one thinks once again of the Halifax explosion prominent in *Barometer Rising* and briefly but significantly alluded to here [211-12]). MacLennan, who was preoccupied with the position of Canada as a nation all his life, is clearly retelling that story here, albeit in indirect form.

Even more compelling than a historical reading, however, is what might be called the existential interpretation of this section. Here Jerome, like George in the rest of the novel, is seen as an Everyman figure living through his representative version of the basic story of modern man. The terms of Jerome's story almost inevitably evoke this kind of reading. At the critical climax in the lumber camp, he is revealed as essentially alone, bereft of parents, society, or any kind of aid beyond his own resources. (MacLennan is here following the example of Dickens, whose numerous orphan or near-orphan figures — Oliver Twist, David Copperfield, Esther Summerson, Pip, and many more — are presented in much the same way as emblems of existential aloneness.) The river image invites allegorical reference, and it is worthwhile noting that at least two critics themselves representing diametrically opposed literary-critical approaches, D.J. Dooley and Robin Mathews, both refer to Jerome embarking "on the river of life" (Dooley 84; Mathews 72).

Moreover, MacLennan clearly endorses this particular way of reading this section, since he employs the image of the canoe in subsequent chapters of the novel to direct attention to its more general significance. I intend now to jump forward for a moment to pick up some of these references. Just before Jerome leaves for Spain, George returns to their summer cottage, and one of the first things he notices is "the red flank of Jerome's beached canoe" (263). This is not just a piece of casual descriptive detail (though it seems to contain a personal memory, since Dorothy Duncan records MacLennan in the 1940s "paddling ... in his red canoe" during their summers "in an old cottage in one of the eastern townships of Quebec" [39]). More importantly, the image foreshadows the fact that Jerome is about to depart on another, even more perilous journey. In the immediately following conversation, in which Jerome tries to justify his decision to George, the latter suddenly "had a vision of Jerome in his tiny canoe going down the New Brunswick river and of Catherine on the shore trying to beckon him in" (271–72). Later, during his visit to Russia, George thinks of Jerome and sees the pattern of his life as representative of the western world in the thirties: "... I remembered Jerome. The canoe in which he had issued from the forest had now taken him out into the ocean. A canoe in an ocean, at night, with a hurricane rising. Jerome, Myself, Everyone" (289). Jerome's dark journey, then, is not just an exciting episode in the plot; it is an imaginative pattern that raises the whole novel to a higher level of fictional subtlety and significance.

Part 6: A Low Dishonest Decade

The central event in this section is Jerome Martell's decision to go to Spain to assist the Popular Front in the Spanish Civil War. It is an action that contains within itself all sorts of personal, moral, ethical, and political elements, but before we consider some of these it will be necessary to discuss a somewhat contentious matter involving historical sources. Jerome's career from this point in the novel onward is often seen as parallelling that of Norman Bethune, the Canadian medical surgeon who also served in Spain before becoming a culture-hero in China where he died assisting Mao Tse Tung's campaigns against the Japanese forces during the Sino-Japanese War. The most detailed argument in favour of Bethune's providing a model for Jerome has been offered (ironically enough) by a Japanese scholar, Keiichi Hirano. The main points of resemblance are as follows. Bethune is the son and Jerome the stepson of poor missionary families whose names reflect French-Huguenot origins. Both serve and are wounded in the First World War. Both become surgeons of international reputations remarkable for their fiery personalities. Both go to Spain to assist the Loyalist cause, and both return after a year to raise funds for continuing support. Bethune then goes to China, where he dies, while Jerome returns to Spain, though he later ends up in China after suffering under the Nazis and spending some time in Auschwitz.

Hirano's arguments up to this point seem to me convincing, though other commentators have been more skeptical. Peter Buitenhuis reports that MacLennan disclaimed any knowledge of Bethune until he had almost completed the novel (56–57), while Elspeth Cameron has gone so far as to assert: "Certainly, the model was not Dr. Norman Bethune, as has been argued, although the coincidental similarities are many" (*Writer's Life* 283). But the resemblances indicated in the previous paragraph seem too close to have been wholly coincidental. It is difficult to believe that allusions to Bethune's activities did not circulate in Montreal during the 1930s when, it must be remembered, MacLennan was living in the city. We do not have to doubt MacLennan's insistence that he was not conscious of specifically modelling Jerome's career on Bethune's while he was planning the novel, but this does not mean that subliminal recollections of a Montreal doctor's politically committed exploits didn't surface in his memory at an appropriate moment without his being fully aware of their origins. Hirano notes, furthermore, that a biography of Bethune, Ted Allan and Sidney Gordon's *The Scalpel, The Sword*, was published in 1952, just about the time that MacLennan began work on the novel; even if he did not read it, he might well have encountered the main facts in reviews and newspaper accounts. This is, to be sure, speculation, but Bethune is in fact mentioned three times within the text of *The Watch That Ends the Night* (146, 233, 266), and the first of these displays some knowledge of Bethune's work in Spain. All this suggests that Norman Bethune indeed served, at least in some respects, as a rough model for MacLennan's "hero."

Where Hirano goes astray is in his interpretation of MacLennan's use of Bethune as model. Like so many socially committed commentators, he has difficulty in seeing any divergence on MacLennan's part from the facts of Bethune's biography as anything but a distortion or even betrayal of "the real." More seriously, he offers a curious misreading of Jerome's character. He argues, for instance, that, whereas Bethune's wife deserted her husband, Jerome is made to abandon Catherine, and that "this slight deviation is a change for the worse" (129). "Between Jerome and Catherine," he claims "no one would hesitate for a moment to lay the blame on the former" (130). In fact, however, MacLennan goes out of his way, as we shall see, to insist upon the intricacy of Jerome's motives. The point is made early in the novel. All their friends, George records, "blamed Jerome and called Catherine a saint" (34), but George sees that the truth is much more complex than that, and the rest of the novel glosses this complexity. It is not true to say that Jerome goes to Spain "on an impulse" (Hirano 130) or that his action "is more a matter of temperament than of principle" (131). Hirano quotes a number of passages in which Jerome refers to his temperament and impulses but ignores such comments as the following:

> ". . . how can anyone live a private life now? All the hatred and the killing has started again and this time it's a thousand percent worse because the killers understand what they're doing. Anything to break the system that causes these things, George. Anything!" (168)

Or:

> "You think I'm abandoning Sally by leaving for Spain. I tell you, if I don't leave for Spain then I really do abandon her to a future of fascism and concentration camps." (269)

These are powerful arguments. MacLennan has forced Jerome to choose between public and private responsibilities — or, rather, to choose between alternatives in which public and private responsibilities are inextricably entangled. We are free to disagree with his decision, but we are not free to condemn him for acting "on an impulse." MacLennan has created a genuinely complex moral problem here.

Hirano then berates MacLennan for what he calls "downgrading in motives." The charge needs to be quoted at length:

> . . . MacLennan has to add such ingredients as Martell's scandalous affair with one of the nurses (who leaves for Spain on the same ship) and the inevitable clash with his superiors. The impression the readers get is that even if Jerome Martell hadn't left of his own free will, people in Montreal simply wouldn't have tolerated him. He had to leave to get out of hot water. Thus the readers no longer have to worry about the rights and wrongs of the Civil War. Martell's behaviour is made completely under-

standable. He could have gone to help the Falangists [i.e. Fascists] in Spain as far as MacLennan and his readers are concerned. (131)

Notice that Hirano gives the impression (without, to be sure, actually saying so) that Jerome managed a planned getaway with Norah Blackwell, though George asserts — and we have no reason to disbelieve him — that he "clearly did not know she was on board the ship" (282). Notice too that Hirano wants a political tract about "the rights and wrongs of the Civil War," not a novel exploring the agonizing combinations of conflicting motives that lie behind any human action. Jerome's motives are political, ideological, professional, personal, marital, psychological, sexual, all at once. To deny the reality of such a bewildering complexity of contradictory principles and motives is to become hopelessly reductive. As for the final sentence I have quoted, it is simply false. No reader who has responded to the full experience of the text could possibly argue in this way. Here Hirano disqualifies himself from serious attention.

What annoys Hirano, of course (and, given his own evident political commitment, this may be granted as understandable), is that MacLennan presents the returned Jerome as, if not disillusioned with communism, at least transcending it — transformed by some sort of mystical illumination. But even if MacLennan drew, consciously or subconsciously, upon certain aspects of Bethune's life for his presentation of Jerome, this does not mean that the two are identified, or that they ought to be identical. Robin Mathews is much closer to the terms of MacLennan's novel when he explains: "MacLennan has to turn away from Bethune as model; he must because his ideology at the basis of *The Watch That Ends the Night* forces a very different structure to the novel than was present in Bethune's life" (75). I disagree with Mathews when he claims that the "Christian, capitalist West clearly meets with MacLennan's approval" (75-76); on the contrary, he "clearly" regards it with distaste but finds the communist alternative even worse. Mathews, however, unlike Hirano, is reading *The Watch That Ends the Night* as a novel rather than a tract, and his summing-up of the Bethune/Jerome controversy seems to me just:

> The Norman Bethune parallels are only interesting in that they show what aspects of the real-life hero MacLennan had to reject

or transform in his task of revealing the way in which his hero, in philosophically idealist terms, has to elude the vanities of the world and find life in the true reality of the spirit. (76)

Mathews's cadences here suggest traditional religious allegory, and this provides a clue to a possible reading of the text at this point. If we are inclined (as, whatever Hirano says, we surely must be) to take Jerome's arguments seriously when he explains why he feels bound to leave for Spain, we are nonetheless likely to feel uneasy. Is he not salving his conscience at the expense of his responsibilities to his wife and child? And if we experience a vague sense of déjà vu here, it may well be because in many respects MacLennan's scene echoes one from John Bunyan's *Pilgrim's Progress*. Close to the beginning of the book, Christian (though his name is not revealed until a little later) has asked the desperate question "What shall I do to be saved?" and has been advised by a guide named Evangelist to fly from the wrath to come and seek only the city of God. There follows this passage:

> So I saw in my dream that the man began to run. Now, he had not run far from his own door, but his wife and children perceiving it, began to cry after him to return; but the man put his fingers in his ears, and ran on, crying Life! life! eternal life! (Luke xiv. 26) So he looked not behind him, but fled towards the middle of the plain (Genesis xix. 17). (1.1857)

It is a passage which embodies a painful collision of values. Bunyan, an eloquent representative of that hard Puritan tradition which MacLennan both challenged and upheld, does not simplify our moral dilemmas. If we are to be saved, we must save ourselves.

This is, in essence, the moral problem that MacLennan raises at this point in his novel. His frequent reference to Everyman, which draws attention to the representativeness of the narrative, encourages this kind of reading. Nonetheless, while I believe this to be a valid interpretation, it is not the only one. Indeed, if we approach this section with some awareness of the history of fiction, we soon realize that MacLennan is also writing within the "great tradition" (as F.R. Leavis christened it) of the nineteenth-century novel. This is a type of fiction in which characters are faced with intricate moral situations reflecting the complex conditions of real life. They are not straightforward matters of right and wrong, to which standard religious or moral apothegms ("thou shalt not steal," "love thy neighbour," "do as you would be done by") easily apply. Often they involve choices between two wrongs, or decisions that result, however one acts, in someone else being hurt. Our judgements in such situations must be governed by an awareness of the complex web of factors that becomes distressingly entangled.

Jerome's dilemma — should he go to Spain or not? — is an excellent example of this kind of painful moral choice. He has obviously reached a critical point in his life: his political principles, his latent religious imperatives, his professional situation, his personal duties and responsibilities, his sexual temptations, all combine, intertwine, and conflict. At the beginning of the section, George provides a cogent account of the way such elements tended to become fused in the troubled 1930s:

> This was a time in which you were always meeting people who caught politics just as a person catches religion. It was probably the last time in this century when politics in our country will be evangelical, and if a man was once intensely religious, he was bound to be wide open to a mood like that of the Thirties. But why waste time explaining the pattern? It is obvious now, and dozens of books have been written about it. Less obvious have been some of the attendant passions that went along with this neo-religious faith. Passion has a way of spilling over into all aspects of the human mind and feelings. It is the most dangerous thing in the world whether it focuses itself on love, religion, reform, politics or art. (223-24)

Because this is a novel about the way in which the lives of private individuals are caught up in the threatening movements of history, we are shown all these elements interrelating — and conflicting — in the life of Jerome. If he attends to what he considers his political duty, he will seem to be abandoning those he loves most; if he remains faithful to the little world of his family, he will be going against the deepest urgings of his conscience. But even that formulation of Jerome's dilemma is too simple. MacLennan knows that no course of action is clear cut and that no motives on any side are totally pure. Hirano criticizes the introduction of complicating elements —

Jerome's guilt over his actions in the First World War, the hostility of his hospital superiors that leads to his resignation, the liaison with Norah Blackwell — as simultaneously simplifying his decision and tainting his association with the communist cause. But that is not so. The Spanish Civil War and the whole situation in Europe are consequences of the actions and passions first released in all their destructive fury in 1914; Jerome's resignation from the hospital occurs in the wake of rebuke after he has publicly demonstrated his political commitments in Montreal; Norah Blackwell is a sexual temptation which Jerome believes he is escaping rather than pursuing in going to Spain — and represents, in any case, the inevitable obverse to Jerome's original decision, as a man of enormous energy, in marrying a known invalid. In creating this intricate situation, MacLennan is attesting to the impossibility of judging in simple terms, whether of straightforward moral right and wrong or of conflicting political ideologies.

This complexity has literary-critical as well as moral consequences, and these are reflected in the attempts of various commentators to come to terms with Jerome as a character. If we see Jerome as "hero," then our responses to him should, according to mythic and literary tradition, be positive — wholly so if we think in the simplistic terms of hero versus villain, predominantly so if we are interested in the flawed tragic hero, more sinned against than sinning. But Jerome doesn't seem to fit into these patterns. For Robin Mathews, he can be seen "as MacLennan's archetypal searcher for truth — at the same time as he may be seen, for much of the novel, as a most deluded person" (71). For Patricia Morley he is "a destroyer as well as a healer; he is not put forward as a purely admirable character" (84–85). What is impressive about MacLennan's art here is his capacity to make us aware of the pros and cons, the strengths and weaknesses, the heroism and the irresponsibility of Jerome "at the same time" (to repeat Mathews's inconspicuous but essential phrase). When we hear of his lightning courtship of Catherine — his insistence that she shall have a child despite the warnings of the other doctors — we recognize this as simultaneously courageous and foolhardy. When he appears at the Pro-Loyalist rally, we can applaud his principles and also regret his naivety and tactlessness. When he decides to go to Spain, we can respect his conscientious need to become involved even as we recognize what he understands only later: that he is also running away from himself, finding lofty reasons to indulge a selfish heroism.

Jerome's heroism is presented, I suggest, as deliberately equivocal. MacLennan may be seen as conducting an inquiry into the possibility of heroism within the contemporary world. In her article "Of Cabbages and Kings: The Concept of the Hero in *The Watch That Ends the Night*," Elspeth Cameron has examined in considerable detail his changing responses to the heroic during the period in which he was writing the novel. She shows how his attitude accompanies a continuing but radical reassessment of the work of Ernest Hemingway, to which he had responded positively in the 1920s. What had once been enthusiasm for a rebellious originality turned first to bitter rejection and then to an uneasy suspicion of what MacLennan came to identify as an irresponsible nihilism — hence the critical references to Hemingway, already noted, within the body of the novel (20, 86).

By the 1950s, Cameron observes, MacLennan was torn between two notions of the heroic: "On the one hand, he greatly admired sheer physical strength, but on the other hand, he respected moral strength, a strength of character which might be termed stoic" (115). Here we see clearly enough the lineaments of Jerome Martell and George Stewart respectively. At the same time, Cameron quotes an important statement by MacLennan tucked away in an obscure article published in the *Montrealer*: "heroes can exist only when men have some fairly clear idea of what they think life ought to be" (qtd. in "Cabbages" 119). Obviously the 1930s was not such a time. This helps us, I think, to see how MacLennan works out his ideas within the form of his novel. The larger-than-life Jerome, a hero in the traditional sense, fits readily enough into those areas of the novel that are closest to "romance" (part 5, for instance), but is an uncomfortable figure — I would argue, a deliberately uncomfortable figure — elsewhere. In those sections of the novel that conform to the nineteenth-century mode of moral realism, George Stewart is the more appropriate central character. George, therefore, is the novel's hero in the literary sense of the term, "the principal male character in a story." But there is even a hint that George may qualify in a modern version of the more traditional sense. To quote Cameron once again: "It was now the ordinary man, the 'little man' ... that typified [the] 1950s" ("Cabbages" 120). This is a matter to which we shall return in the next section.

It was W.H. Auden who referred to the 1930s, in a famous phrase from a later-rejected poem, "September 1, 1939," as "a low dishonest decade" (98). MacLennan presents it, from the perspective of Montreal, in all its infuriating shabbiness, inconsistency, and self-deception. From the middle-of-the-road and therefore somewhat limited viewpoint of George Stewart, we are introduced to a considerable range of characters representative in both class and temperament, from the manipulating businessmen Huntley McQueen and Sir Rupert Irons (108, 139) — both of whom had already made appearances in *Two Solitudes* — through bemused administrators like Dr. Rodgers to the intellectual left-wingers like John David and Arthur Lazenby and such rank-and-file as Norah and Harry Blackwell. Inevitably, judgements on such presentations differ. Stanley Ryerson sees in the presentation of the Left in the novel only "a gratuitous lampoon on their worst sectarian failings" (15); on the other hand, George Woodcock, hardly a stranger to the politics of protest, even if his own 1930s experience was in England rather than in Canada, can write: "anyone who lived through the Thirties will have met the prototypes of Norah Blackwell, Arthur Lazenby and Adam Blore" (*Hugh MacLennan* 108–09). Once again it is important to insist that the perspective is that of an uninfluential segment of the middle class unimpressed by the assumptions and tactics of either extreme.

Woodcock has also referred to *The Watch That Ends the Night* as MacLennan's "most successful social novel" (100), a phrase that seems to me misleading in general, though there are certainly sections of part 6 that go some way towards justifying it. One of these is the vivid account of the violence at the pro-Loyalist rally, where MacLennan not only provides an insight into the ideological tensions of the period, in the tradition of the "social novel," but also communicates dramatically what it feels like to be caught up in such an event. The fictional scene is thoroughly realized in its own right and needs no buttressing from external sources, but it is worth pointing out that MacLennan based his account on a historical incident. Ben-Zion Shek made the connection at the 1982 MacLennan conference:

> I believe the fictionalized incident was based on a real one — the visit to Quebec by André Malraux who was collecting funds for the Republican cause. A meeting addressed by Malraux was in fact broken up by francophone students, and their action was publicly defended by Cardinal Villeneuve who stated that the

law of nature superseded other laws, and made nought of the
alleged threat of fascism. (130)

MacLennan was in the audience and, when Shek asked him if he had
this incident in mind, replied: "Yes, exactly" (131).

Another event with, this time, an autobiographical origin is George
Stewart's trip to Russia. MacLennan had been on a similar visit under
similar circumstances. He went, as Cameron records in her biography, in a mood of deep dissatisfaction with the situation in North
America, and prepared "to find a brave new world." He returned
disillusioned, convinced that Stalin had betrayed the revolution: " 'I
would say that 90% of what I understood to be communist theories
... have been scrapped, at least for the time being' " (qtd. in *Writer's
Life* 116). Others, as Cameron notes, had made visits to Russia
without experiencing this violent reaction, including Norman
Bethune; however, the revelations concerning life under Stalin that
have come from Russia in the years since *The Watch That Ends the
Night* was published show MacLennan's judgement to have been
shrewd.

This incident is not, however, included in the novel purely for
ideological reasons. No critic, so far as I can remember, has noted
how MacLennan skillfully echoes here his description of the Montreal unemployed that I quoted earlier (see pp. 67–68). In Leningrad,
he hears "the perpetual rustling of thousands of shoeless feet." The
smock-wearing crowds "flowed hour after hour without ceasing
because, apparently, they had nothing else to do and no place to go."
Their feet were "wrapped in bandages and hemp because there were
not enough shoes in Russia, and because the price of a pair of cheap
shoes cost more than double the monthly pay of the average Soviet
worker that year" (285, 286). The shoes of the Montreal poor, we
may remember, were only "cheap" and "worn." The point may have
been missed by the literary critics, but it seems to have got under the
skin of the Canadian Left. Thus Ryerson, criticizing MacLennan's
presentation of Montreal, remarks: "one gets an impression of permanently passive, faceless unemployed persons, the sound of their
feet 'shuffling' (the word recurs) along St. Catherine Street being
well-nigh the sum-total of their presence" (15). We shall look in vain
for any "shuffling" in the Montreal scenes; "the word recurs," to be
sure, but only in the description of the peasants in Leningrad! The

incident would be merely amusing (in a sour sort of way) if it did not throw an oblique and unintentional ray of light upon MacLennan's quiet artistry.

Part 7: *The Courage To Be*

In the final section of *The Watch That Ends the Night*, we encounter in its most urgent form a problem that arises at some point in the discussion of any MacLennan novel: the problem of didacticism. To what extent is it permissible to grant a teaching function to a work of fiction? The official tendency in the twentieth century has been to regard didacticism in any work of art as some sort of offence against its aesthetic purity. Many Canadian writers of a later generation than MacLennan uphold this attitude. "No lessons. No lessons *ever*," exclaims Alice Munro when an interviewer asks about "a message coming across" in her work (Hancock 222–23). John Metcalf is suspicious of any literary work which "bulges with undigested chunks of 'something to say' " (48). It is in this sense that Donald Cameron, in a foreword to Cockburn's book, used the phrase "ruinously didactic" in connection with MacLennan's fiction.

This has not, however, been an attitude held in earlier historical periods. The Roman poet Horace (and we should remember once again that MacLennan began as a student of the classics) wrote in his *Ars Poetica* of the artist's responsibility to teach and to delight, and this view of the matter remained dominant until recent times. Charles Dickens, for instance, frequently used his fiction to draw attention to social abuses — the workhouse system in *Oliver Twist*, conditions in unregulated boarding schools in *Nicholas Nickleby*, the labyrinth of the law in *Bleak House*, etc. Some works, notably Harriet Beecher Stowe's *Uncle Tom's Cabin*, have been directly influential in altering popular attitudes to social questions, while in the twentieth century others, like D.H. Lawrence's, have more obliquely caused public questioning on issues such as class and sex. In recent Canadian literature, didacticism in fiction has tended to take the form of satirical parody of absurdities (in the work of Robertson Davies and Margaret Atwood, for example) or of drawing attention to the problems of minorities (Rudy Wiebe's novels on Mennonites and Métis, Mordecai Richler's on Jewish life and attitudes). Indeed, most serious fiction may be said to be at least implicitly didactic if it attempts to reflect the conditions of contemporary life. Thus, while one doesn't think of Margaret Laurence or Alice Munro as didactic writers, their sympathetic presentation of women's viewpoints has been influential in recent years without being either militantly feminist or conspicuously instructive.

But the work of Hugh MacLennan has been didactic in a more obvious way. George Woodcock has written well on this subject in the section entitled "The Didactic Urge" in a companion volume to this one, *Introducing Hugh MacLennan's Barometer Rising*. As he notes, MacLennan's didacticism often takes the form of a nationalistic stance. He set out, as it were, to put Canada on the fictional map, and sometimes his generalizations about things Canadian interrupt the fictional section and seem unduly intrusive. This happens occasionally in *The Watch That Ends the Night* — towards the end of part 6, for example, when George writes:

> While the war thundered on, Canada unnoticed grew into a nation at last. This cautious country which had always done more than she had promised, had always endured in silence while others reaped the glory — now she became alive and to us within her excitingly so. (317)

These sound more like Hugh MacLennan's sentiments than George Stewart's; certainly, they are only indirectly connected with the more universal issues that have concerned George for most of the book. In such passages, we may well feel that the didactic element intrudes too conspicuously. It has not been sufficiently integrated into the fictional action.

The major didactic problem in this novel, however, is of a different kind. The religious crisis that forms the climax to *The Watch That Ends the Night* involves matters more commonly treated in non-fiction discourse: matters of belief in God, the meaning (or meaninglessness) of suffering, the nature of death, and so on. When MacLennan begins a chapter with the sentence, "I can continue with this story and make sense of what follows only if I succeed in explaining something very difficult" (340), it is as if the fiction has stopped and some form of non-fiction writing has taken its place. This whole chapter reads like a personal confession, a deeply felt statement by one who has lived and suffered greatly. It is, of course, precisely that, and whether the speaking voice is the fictional George Stewart or that of MacLennan himself hardly seems to matter very much.

Artistically, however, the effect raises problems, and many commentators have criticized the novel at this point. For Hugo McPherson the novel's "freight of didactic commentary is unnecessarily bulky; one feels, indeed, that the essayist at this point is crowding out the novelist — that MacLennan is ultimately more comfortable with discursive argument than with dramatic rendering" (702). W.H. New remarks that "a tendency to wordiness accompanies MacLennan's difficulty in voicing the paradox of which he has become aware" (32). Peter Buitenhuis goes further: "In the last section of the book, the narrator's voice becomes less authentic. MacLennan seems to lose the ironic distance which had separated him from George during the major part of the novel. . . . The author's voice comes through too insistently, and the illusion of the novel collapses among a heap of morals" (64). Speaking for myself, I understand the reasoning behind such criticisms; indeed, my whole literary training tells me that I ought to agree. But the ultimate test is surely the experience of reading, and honesty requires me to acknowledge that, whenever I read the book, I find this section as deeply moving, as emotionally compelling, as any piece of writing that I know. In other words, my emotional response is in conflict with my intellectual theory, and I have become firmly convinced that in such cases it is the intellectual theory that must give way.

The main problem, as MacLennan knew very well, is that he was feeling his way towards levels of experience that ultimately take him beyond the limits of language. He therefore causes George to remark: "I know my language is not good, it is not scientifically accurate, but it will have to do" (360). And: "Nobody has ever described such a struggle truly in words. Nobody can" (343). In even attempting to express the inexpressible, he is approaching the notorious uncertain territory of the religious mystics. What we encounter at this spiritual climax to the novel is an experience very close to that which St. John of the Cross described as the dark night of the soul, the experience of spiritual dryness which, we are told, all aspiring souls must suffer before attaining unity with the Divine. George must win through to a position in which he can display, in Paul Tillich's well-known phrase, "the courage to be" (I have been anticipated, in applying this phrase to MacLennan's novel, by D.J. Dooley [90]). MacLennan is writing within this mystical/literary tradition when, like so many visionary writers, he falls back on the language of paradox in an attempt to communicate a moment of intense insight:

> This, which is darkness, also is light. This, which is no, also is yes. This, which is hatred, also is love. This, which is fear, also is courage. This, which is defeat, also is victory. (344)

It is impossible to deny that something has broken here. Fiction has collapsed, but not, I think, as Buitenhuis claims, in "a heap of morals"; rather, it has collapsed into the direct mode of the personal essay. Art has here abandoned its ideal of aesthetic detachment to engage in the pressing concerns of life. The novel is now revealed as more than a book about people who lived and suffered through the troubled years of the mid-twentieth century: it has become a book about each and every one of us.

In addition, I would submit that the standard procedures of literary criticism have to be abandoned at this point. The purist will see this as a betrayal, continuing to invoke the criteria that work with more conventional novels, but we might do well to consider the possibility that MacLennan is involved in a deliberate and boldly experimental effect designed to challenge our tendency to locate art and life in conveniently separate categories. In these final pages, George recognizes himself as Everyman (a term, it needs to be said now, that includes "Everywoman"; in the 1950s the word was generally accepted, without question and without awkwardness, as embracing all human beings). But this leads to a further mysterious — or mystical — paradox: "All of us is Everyman and this is intolerable unless each of us can also be I" (367). Here MacLennan's readers ("us") are invited to become part of the equation, to cease reading the novel as the presentation of an action remote from their experience but to recognize the pattern of George's experience as mirroring the circumstances of all their lives. When George is able to confront "the human plight" (344), the boundaries of fiction, of narrative artifice, have long been transcended. This leads, however, to yet another paradox, the realization that "the human bondage is also the human liberty" (344).

At this point, then, we need to rethink any assumptions we may have about aesthetic distance. That the author should remain detached from his or her first-person narrator is a generally held literary-critical principle, but few principles are without their exceptions and it is possible that this one should, in certain cases, be challenged. Paul Goetsch remarks: "In the final part of the novel, ... MacLennan seems to identify himself so much with the narrator that many readers will find Stewart's remarks, rhetorical and painfully emotional as they are, hard to accept" ("Too Long" 28). One wonders, however, whether this ought not, logically, to make the remarks harder to *reject*, since they reflect the author's experience as well as the narrator's. The closeness of George Stewart's experience to MacLennan's, of Catherine's to Dorothy Duncan's, may now be seen as an advantage rather than a liability. We are prepared to listen to George's account of his painful coming to terms with Catherine's situation, of his learning the meaning of Jerome's mysterious injunction to let her "live her own death" (364), because we are now aware that George speaks out of his creator's authority and experience. Artistic skill and dexterity have achieved their purpose — and are, of course, still evident in various forms as the narrative proceeds — but MacLennan as visionary author has now passed beyond them. The fictional has blended inextricably with the real. If as readers we began with a willing suspension of disbelief, we end in experiential acceptance. Walt Whitman's comment in "So Long!" is profoundly applicable here: "This is no book; / Who touches this touches a man" (345).

MacLennan is leading us into strange country in the concluding pages of this novel, past a psychological border point (the image of frontiers is recurrent throughout the book) where fiction, history, sociopolitical commentary, and autobiographical memoir meet. George Stewart may now be seen, at one and the same time, as a central character within the novel, an ordinary man within the real world tossed hither and yon by the implacable forces of history, a personal essayist with a deeply individual viewpoint, and a mask for Hugh MacLennan recounting the painful but ennobling final years of his first marriage. Yet, however much MacLennan may have broken down the generic boundaries that conventionally separate different kinds of writing, he is still concerned with fulfilling his commitment to tell the story that he promised in the opening words of the novel. Despite the religious and spiritual revelations of the conclusion, and their urgent application to the world his readers inhabit, he is still aware of the demands of fictional form.

At the very time that he is breaking down the barriers that separate author from narrator, he is simultaneously drawing attention to the resemblances that bind character to character. These structural links are implied throughout the book, but they become especially conspicuous as it draws towards its close. Just before part 7 begins, George quotes John Donne's famous phrase, "no man is an island entire of itself" (323). The evidence for this has been steadily mounting through part 6. When Catherine talks to George about Jerome, she admits: " 'I've battened on him too much. . . . I made him my whole life' " (241). We are inevitably reminded of George's early acknowledgement that he had made Catherine his "rock" (6). Catherine, indeed, goes even further and later admits to George: " 'I've done to you what Norah Blackwell did to Jerome' " (314). Moreover, George himself comes to realize that, however far he may be from Jerome in many respects, they too have their interconnections: "I remembered Jerome in his canoe going down the river to the sea, and my thought that at last he had reached the sea and was out of sight of land in his canoe. Now I, too, was at sea . . ." (315).

These interconnections become even more evident in part 7. At this point George realizes that Jerome and Catherine share a common pattern. In an eloquent one-sentence paragraph early in the first chapter of this section he remarks: "You see, Jerome — like Catherine — had returned from the dead" (328). Such links are transformed into something close to allegorical structure in the scene — the first occasion on which the two men meet face to face in the "present" of the novel — where George and Jerome meet in the hospital: "and so after all those years we two met again with Catherine's small, silent body between us" (361). The bold patterning of "romance" is once again evident here: a contrived situation, to be sure, but an appropriate one for the protagonist to enter on the final stage of his understanding. And here Jerome admits, in response to George's charge that he abandoned Catherine when going to Spain: " 'Actually, I think I was doing what you're trying to do now. I was running away from myself, not from her' " (363).

Some ideological critics (notably Keiichi Hirano) have interpreted this scene as MacLennan's own abandonment of political concern, as a betrayal of the political commitment described in parts 4 and 6. But it is nothing of the sort. MacLennan is not *substituting* this motive for those that Jerome offered to George at the close of part 6 (see

168). He is insisting that any human decision is made as the result of a tissue of conflicting motives. He is here restating in psychological terms what he had previously stated in political ones. No human motive is totally pure, and MacLennan presents the deeply personal determinants of Jerome's action not to detract from his political sincerity but to set it within a broader and more intricate context of values. This is in line with the argument that George has been making throughout the book — that individual action is determined by a complex set of interrelating but often conflicting motives that can never be wholly disentangled. Indeed, what we are seeing in these closing chapters of the novel is the process by which George comes to his insights into human behaviour — a phenomenon that can never be separated from a recognition of human mystery. Out of the understanding that George gains here, in his own personal life, come the motives — almost, one might say, the justification — for the whole commentary.

The novel is clearly drawing towards its close. The two main time schemes juxtaposed in the earlier sections of the novel have now come together; in the final chapter of part 6, the retrospective account of the past finally catches up with the novel's present. With the resolution obviously close at hand, and the inevitable death of Catherine imminent, we may detect a serious tension here on the part of George — and, perhaps, of MacLennan. The novel will stand or fall by the success or failure of the climax to which the whole narrative has been moving. As I remarked at the opening of this commentary, few would deny that *The Watch That Ends the Night* contains blemishes, and it would be foolish to attempt to deny them. The first chapter of part 7 begins somewhat awkwardly since George has to construct an account of Jerome's movements on the days immediately following his return to Montreal, and then to recount the scene of Jerome's visit to Catherine which George did not, of course, witness. A similar difficulty occurs in the seventh chapter where Harry Blackwell encounters Jerome. There is no problem concerning George's subsequent hearing of accounts of these events, but a certain formal artificiality, alien to the rest of the novel, is nonetheless detectable.

Another difficulty occurs when Jerome describes his religious conversion. The truths that MacLennan is concerned with here are doubtless universal, but any expression of them must conform to a particular (and therefore limiting) cultural form. Any specificity, any favouring of one set of values over another, can threaten to detract from the novel's effectiveness. Above all, any tendency towards overt sermonizing is likely to alienate. Given the official, albeit retreating, Christian context in which MacLennan found himself, it was natural enough that he should be drawn towards specifically Christian references. In my view, however, some of these jar. Take, for instance, the direct speech in which Jerome addresses Catherine:

> "One day I woke up and Jesus himself seemed to be in the cell with me and I wasn't alone. He wasn't anyone I had ever known before. He wasn't the Jesus of the churches. He wasn't the Jesus who had died for our sins. He was simply a man who had died and risen again. Who had died outwardly as I had died inwardly." (329–30)

The opening sentence is surely too bald, too easy; it recalls too many dubious conversion stories in the more naïve evangelizing Christian tradition. Moreover, it seems to be attempting to have its cake and eat it: if this Jesus isn't "the Jesus of the churches" or "the Jesus who had died for our sins," in what sense is he Jesus at all? And what precisely is the meaning of the sentence, "He was *simply* a man who had died and risen again"? At this moment, it is difficult not to accept Patricia Merivale's seemingly harsh phrasing when she argues that Jerome "comes back from the dead after World War 11 with a rather implausible line in saintliness" (60).

Such weaknesses need to be acknowledged. At the same time, they should not blind us to the many notable strengths of this section. Not least of these is the way certain new words take the place of others that had become recurrent motifs in the earlier parts of the novel. One of these, a bold stroke on MacLennan's part, is "hate." When blaming Jerome for Catherine's latest embolism, George admits that he "hated him and wanted to kill him" (355). As he walks down the hospital corridor to encounter Jerome at Catherine's bedside, he confesses: "I hated them both — Catherine no less than Jerome. I hated myself and I hated life" (360). And a little later, he accuses Jerome of hating Catherine for offering her a few more years of life as an invalid (363). "This, which is hatred, also is love" (344), he has remarked in the list of paradoxes already quoted. It is to

MacLennan's credit that he does not flinch from presenting these darker impulses (though Robertson Davies goes too far, I think, in interpreting Catherine as a "spiritual vampire" [121] — MacLennan acknowledges the "battening" quality, recognizes her manipulation of her illness to obtain what she wants, without turning her into a monster). Besides, the emphasis on "hate" is balanced by a new emphasis on words like "light" and "joy" and "mystery." Catherine's late-developing talent for painting, a characteristic borrowed from Dorothy Duncan, is a thematic equivalent of these verbal paradoxes: creativity manifesting itself under the shadow of death. It would be a mistake to let MacLennan's occasional lapses detract from the successful effects that he achieves (I am tempted to say, triumphantly) against the grain of his age.

To conclude my discussion of this section, I would like to draw attention to one of MacLennan's minor but, I think, characteristic technical strokes: his introduction, so late in the novel, of the taxi-driver Romeo Pronovost. He is the last of what I have called MacLennan's Dickensian figures — almost a caricature, but warmly comic and, I would argue, profoundly relevant to MacLennan's main concern at this point in the novel. Pronovost is a master of the obvious: "he gave it as his opinion that sickness was a terrible thing for sure.... '*Le bon Dieu a des idées très singulières*' " (348; [the good God has very strange ideas]). His language never rises above cliché — "All you got to do is smell, he said, and you smell the spring in the air" (359) — and cliché, indeed, provides the clue. MacLennan is acutely aware in this section of the danger yet at the same time the inevitability of cliché. He makes this clear when Jerome asserts that George is not so much afraid of death as afraid of life. George comments: "I had said to myself before that perhaps I was afraid of life. It was an old cliché — to be afraid of life. Now I looked at him and I knew that it was more than a cliché" (366). MacLennan makes a similar point in creating Pronovost as a conduit for everyday cliché. If George is at times close to cliché, to the "complacencies" that bothered Warren Tallman, he shows us in the honest and admirable taxi driver what complacency and banality — however they may coexist with goodness and decency — actually sound like. But Pronovost, for all his comic simplicity, is right: sickness *is* a terrible thing; God *does* work in mysterious ways; and, above all, he anticipates Catherine's temporary survival by smelling "spring in the air."

But Pronovost also serves a somewhat different if related function. He is, one is tempted to say, the archetype of "the little man," and the little man becomes an important factor at this stage in the narrative. At a crucial point in his spiritual crisis, George quotes, "Little man, what now?" (343) — a reference, as Elspeth Cameron reminds us, to a once well-known humorous book by Rudolf Ditzen (*Writer's Life* 258). Harry Blackwell (whose reappearance in this section is thematically significant) is another "little man," and is specifically described as such (355). And George Stewart knows that, for all his education, his professional status, his reputation as radio-commentator, he too is a little man in a world of uncontrollable forces that seem to dwarf all human initiative. And here we are reminded of Cameron's remark I have already quoted: "It was now the ordinary man, the 'little man' ... that typified [the] 1950s" ("Cabbages" 120). As Jerome, the larger-than-life, increasingly incongruous "hero" passes out of the story (" 'I won't come back here again, George' " [368]), the little man takes centre stage. And he is not to be treated lightly or condescendingly. MacLennan is obviously amused by Pronovost, but he leaves us in no doubt about his qualities. George remarks: "His eyes looked into mine, and for an instant the man's goodness reached me and made me feel, for an instant, pure" (348). At the climax of *The Watch That Ends the Night*, because in the modern world the ordinary business of living becomes a feat of constant struggle and endurance, the good "little men" — Pronovost, George, and let us hope, ourselves — have become, in a new sense, heroic.

Epilogue: Into Mystery

MacLennan's Epilogue — a kind of coda to the novel as a whole — is brief, and commentary upon it can also be brief. The action is over; the chapter exists in a limbo as both George and Catherine learn to glory in the short span of life that is left to them together. Part of it takes place in "the cathedral hush of a Quebec Indian summer" (372), and it is itself an Indian summer — or, perhaps, the last watch before the night. The key word is now "mystery." "*Omnia exeunt in mysteria,*" we are told (372; [all things pass into mystery]). The wisdom that comes from this experience is in danger of sounding dubiously uplifting:

> ... to be able to love the mystery surrounding us is the final and only sanction of human existence. (372).
> Life was a gift; I knew that now. (372)
> I knew, deep inside, that this struggle was not valueless. (373)

Complacency? Banality? Cliché? Individual readers must make up their own minds. Stephen Bonnycastle, as I have already noted, considers these pages "the finest in the novel," praising MacLennan's "tenderness," "delicacy," and "honesty" in successfully bringing his book, thematically and artistically, to a close (83). I am inclined to agree because these statements have been *earned* by the whole experience of the narrative. Extracted from their context, as I have extracted them here, may well make them seem excessively didactic. But we have spent close to four hundred pages with George Stewart as he wrestles with the problems of life and the confrontation with death. This epilogue records his successful emergence on the other side of the dark night of the soul. Bonnycastle remarks — justly, I think — that his "assertions are much more guarded than is common in religious discourse, and they are the more exhilarating for that" (82). We may at the very least acknowledge, surely, that they constitute "more than a cliché" (366).

MacLennan's final effect is to leave us with a curiously indeterminate sense of time. On the final page, he invokes for the last time the somewhat dour image of "the ocean of time" that "overwhelms us all." He then launches — some might say, a little blatantly — into Jesus's parable of the talents as recorded in St. Matthew's gospel (25.14–23), ending: "Enter thou into the joy of the Lord." The next paragraph begins: "So, in the end, did Catherine" — which seems to suggest that at this point Catherine dies. But this is not in fact so; for MacLennan, "the joy of the Lord" refers to the temporary respite of peace and joy that they discover within this world. Nonetheless, George's future — and Catherine's death — must be faced: "Later, when the time came when I would have to continue alone, later would be the time for the prayer I knew she hoped would be answered: *nunc requiesce in me*" (373; [now rest in me]).

Thomas Hardy once remarked that every deathbed becomes the fifth act of a tragedy, but the status of tragedy in the century of "the little man" has been much debated. True tragedy, we remember, is exalting as well as chastening, a triumph as well as a loss. As I come to the end of a reading of this book, which I have read many times, I am invariably convinced that, if tragic emotion is possible in the literature of the modern world, it is attained in *The Watch That Ends the Night.*

Postscript: HUGH MACLENNAN AND ROBERTSON DAVIES

In the section entitled "Critical Reception," I referred to Robertson Davies's favourable and thoughtful review of *The Watch That Ends the Night* which appeared soon after the book's first publication in 1959. Eleven years later, after a long absence as a novelist, Davies initiated a new stage in his own literary career with *Fifth Business*, which later became the first novel in his Deptford Trilogy. At first sight, the contrast between the two books seems extreme: MacLennan offers an account of human endurance and an agonizing search for spiritual understanding and fulfilment in mid-century Montreal, while Davies tells a tale of magic, wonder, and generally bizarre doings that result from a boy's throwing of a snowball in an Ontario small town. On further investigation, however, some profound resemblances become manifest. Patricia Merivale, in an article entitled "The (Auto)-Biographical Compulsions of Dunstan Ramsay," has examined the interconnections in detail, and even characterizes *Fifth Business* as "a conscious tribute to and a subversive spoof of MacLennan's book" (62). Personally, I would not go quite so far as that. But the suggestion is an intriguing one. To consider the ways in which MacLennan's seemingly traditional novel became an inspiration for a well-known and at least superficially more original Canadian novel published a decade later will be an appropriate way to bring this discussion of *The Watch That Ends the Night* to a close.

It seems as if Davies was deeply influenced by MacLennan's blending of realistic reportage with the recognition of recurring mythic patterns and shrewd psychological probing. There is no question of Davies in any way imitating MacLennan. Rather, what seems to have happened is that the impact of *The Watch That Ends the Night* stayed with him, at some unconscious level, during the 1960s when circumstances prevented him from devoting himself to another novel. When the opportunity eventually occurred, many of MacLennan's themes and effects reappeared, duly transformed by Davies's highly individual fictional talent. *Fifth Business* is an achieved work of fiction in its own right, and one that is the subject of a companion study in this Canadian Fiction Studies series. All the more reason, then, to investigate some of the curious interrelationships between the two books.

We may start with the observation that Davies's perceptive comment on *The Watch That Ends the Night* in his review — "the story-teller and the self-explorer are one" (120) — could apply with equal aptness to his own Dunstan Ramsay. Similarly, a shrewd comment in the second Deptford novel, *The Manticore* — "The modern hero is the man who conquers in the inner struggle" (295) — would provide an illuminating gloss on the story of George Stewart. Davies, as is well known, has long been a devoted follower of the psychologist Carl Jung, and it may well be that he recognized in MacLennan's work a pattern of human development that seemed deeply relevant to Jung's psychological theories. Long before the publication of the Deptford Trilogy, indeed, the critic Paul Goetsch had suggested that *The Watch That Ends the Night* might be usefully interpreted "as analogous to Jung's analytic technique — as an individuation process, in which the contents of the unconscious is assimilated with the conscious to effect a harmonization of the psyche" ("Too Long" 26).

Let us look at some of the interconnections between the two novels a little more closely. Both protagonists are teachers of history (both, indeed, gained degrees in history from the University of Toronto), and both have their own individual attitudes to the historical process. George Stewart comes to see the forces that determine history as mysterious, irrational, and uncontrollable. Since power has now passed to the scientists, politicians are no longer "genuine makers of history" and must now realize that "control was out of their hands" (37). He disagrees with those who still consider politics "a rational occupation," seeing international crises as matters of "obscure and absolutely irrational passions" whose causes develop slowly and inexorably until they result in "explosion" (245). Dunstan Ramsay's motives for studying history after his experiences in the First World War are remarkably similar: ". . . during my fighting days I had become conscious that I was being used by powers over which I had no control for purposes of which I had no understanding. History, I hoped, would teach me how the world's affairs worked. It never really did so, but I became interested in it for its own sake" (110). Dunstan develops a special interest in the mythic patterns that repeat themselves in various historical situations, while MacLennan's George Stewart comes to recognize such patterns not so much in history itself but as embodied within his own experience.

More specifically, both protagonists are relatively passive characters who tend to define themselves, as it were, by contrast with friends who are dominating men of action, Jerome Martell and Boy Staunton. George Stewart, we might say, is eminently qualified for the role of "Fifth Business," a minor character required for the resolution of a plot, yet, like Dunstan, he emerges as hero in "the inner struggle." Both initially lose out in the sexual triangle, and both project their need for a saint-figure on to women, George on to Catherine, Dunstan, more idiosyncratically, on to Mary Dempster. Patricia Merivale sees both texts as examples of a fictional genre she calls "elegiac romance," in which the narrator tells his own story while recounting that of a heroic and generally dead friend whose influence he transcends "through the very act of narration" (57). The hero, she notes,

> is a little larger than life and more splendid than the conventions of psychological realism encourage, while the narrator subdues his own characterization to those same conventions. We come to see that "the hero," as described to us, is largely a projection into mythic dimensions of the needs and obsessions of his narrator. (58)

There are, of course, certain differences, but even these are often evidence of fascinating interconnections between the texts. In *Fifth Business*, it is the narrator who returns, like MacLennan's hero, from the dead, since he is officially reported as killed in battle. Davies seems to appropriate Martell's experience in the First World War for his historian-narrator. Jerome, in self disgust after having contracted gonorrhea from a casual sexual liaison, tries to get himself killed on the battlefield and instead is awarded the Military Medal for bravery. Dunstan, at this time a sexual innocent, is running confusedly from the centre of a bombardment and, while looking for cover, unintentionally enters a German machine-gun nest. He shoots the three occupants at point-blank range out of desperate self-defence (compare Jerome's bayonetting of eleven Germans), and for this act he is subsequently awarded the Victoria Cross. In this way, Davies complicates the otherwise rather simple pattern of passive narrator and active hero, but it is difficult to avoid the conclusion that, even in his alterations, Davies is in some way following MacLennan's example.

There are many more resemblances that may or may not be coincidental. Sally refers to Alan Royce as "one of our most accomplished swordsmen" (41), and Davies has great fun with the same term in *The Manticore* (187); both note the tendency of left-wingers in the 1930s to refer to "capit'alists" (*Watch* 145; *Fifth Business* 150); Jerome as "divine fool" (297) may even connect with Mary Dempster as "fool-saint" (138–39). Much more significant, however, is the capacity of both writers to create fictions that exist within a kind of no-man's-land between novel and romance — and for a similar reason, since both present their protagonists as fulfilling characteristic patterns of human behaviour, whether mystical or mythic. Davies is, from the start, far more concerned with individual idiosyncrasy and far less with social commitment than MacLennan, but ultimately both work their way through to a view of human life that can legitimately be designated "religious." Or, to put the matter in less dogmatic terms, both are convinced that "God is not mocked" (*Manticore* 206) and that the universe in which we find ourselves reveals a mysterious, ultimately incomprehensible, but nonetheless palpable purpose.

These are not, of course, fashionable sentiments; as a result, neither MacLennan nor Davies fits readily into the mainstream of Canadian literature as it is generally recognized at the present time. Davies is currently more highly regarded than MacLennan because he displays a greater technical inventiveness, though to many (I am not speaking for myself) his ideas and attitudes are considered quaint and even reactionary. MacLennan is a more doubtful case. In the middle years of the century, before the emergence of Margaret Laurence and others in the mid-sixties, he was generally regarded as the most prominent of Canadian novelists. Part of the reason for this was his emphasis on Canadian locales and his fictional treatment of specifically Canadian issues. Ironically, however, while the increased national awareness of the 1960s acknowledged MacLennan's position as a public figure, new standards of literary achievement were beginning to make his fiction appear technically somewhat outmoded. As early as 1969, George Woodcock could describe him as "a writer emphatically, but not necessarily fatally, out of period and fashion" (*Hugh MacLennan* 27).

Judgements on MacLennan's fiction are likely to fluctuate considerably in the near future, since the crucial years so far as a literary reputation is concerned are those immediately following the writer's death. There is a kind of artistic limbo in which an individual's body of work is too old to pass as fully contemporary yet too recent to be read in historical perspective. It seems to me not unlikely that MacLennan's general reputation as a significant literary figure will decline somewhat over the course of time. But *The Watch That Ends the Night* is his least contrived novel, and its combination of documentary vividness and personal urgency ought to cause it to emerge as a book of lasting interest. Another effect of time upon literature is that formal and stylistic quality eventually wins out over the fashionably daring. Indeed, it has been a feature of Canadian literary experience over the last half-century that novels whose authors have fulfilled the terms of their own talent rather than tailoring their work to preconceived models of what is good or acceptable have shown a definite staying power. I am thinking of books like Sheila Watson's *The Double Hook*, Rudy Wiebe's *The Blue Mountains of China*, Hugh Hood's *A New Athens*, Jack Hodgins's *The Invention of the World* — as well, of course, as Davies's *Fifth Business*. Hugh MacLennan's *The Watch That Ends the Night* surely belongs with these. It is difficult to believe that a novel so unequivocally human in its emphasis and concerns will not have something to say to sensitive and thoughtful people at all times.

Works Cited

Auden, W.H. *Another Time: Poems.* New York: Random, 1940.

Blake, William. "The Marriage of Heaven and Hell." *The Norton Anthology of English Literature.* 6th ed. Vol. 2. New York: Norton, 1993.

Blodgett, E.D. "Intertextual Design in Hugh MacLennan's *The Watch That Ends the Night.*" *Canadian Review of Comparative Literature* 5 (1978): 280–88.

    Perceptive discussion of the Odysseus and Oedipus myths, and the writings of Goethe and Rilke in relation to *The Watch.*

Bonnycastle, Stephen. "The Power of *The Watch That Ends the Night.*" *Journal of Canadian Studies* 14.4 (1979–80): 76–89.

    Perhaps the best article on *The Watch*, comparing it to the writings of Wordsworth, Proust, and Spinoza.

Brazeau, Jacques. "Perception du Canada français dans l'oeuvre de Hugh MacLennan." In E. Cameron, *Hugh MacLennan: 1982* 35–47.

Buitenhuis, Peter. *Hugh MacLennan.* Canadian Writers and Their Works. Toronto: Forum, 1969.

    Sensible introductory study up to time of writing, including chapter on *The Watch.*

Bunyan, John. *The Pilgrim's Progress. The Norton Anthology of English Literature.* 6th ed. Vol. 1. New York: Norton, 1993.

Cameron, Donald. "Hugh MacLennan: The Tennis Racket Is an Antelope Bone." *Conversations with Canadian Novelists.* Part One. Toronto: Macmillan, 1973. 130–48.

    Useful interview.

Cameron, Elspeth. "Hugh MacLennan: An Annotated Bibliography." *The Annotated Bibliography of Canada's Major Authors.* Ed. Robert Lecker and Jack David. Vol. 1. Downsview: ECW, 1979. 103–53.

    Invaluable bibliography to time of publication.

———. *Hugh MacLennan: A Writer's Life.* Toronto: U of Toronto P, 1981.

A detailed, readable, indispensable biography.

———, ed. *Hugh MacLennan: 1982*. Toronto: University College, University of Toronto, Canadian Studies Programme, 1982.

Proceedings of a MacLennan conference held at University College in February 1982.

———. "Of Cabbages and Kings: The Concept of the Hero in *The Watch That Ends the Night*." *The Canadian Novel: Modern Times*. Ed. John Moss. Toronto: NC, 1982. 106–29.

Solid account of MacLennan's developing attitudes towards "the hero" during the 1950s.

Cockburn, Robert H. *The Novels of Hugh MacLennan*. Montreal: Harvest, 1969.

A generally unsympathetic study, including chapter on *The Watch*.

Davies, Robertson. *Fifth Business*. 1970. Markham: Penguin, 1983.

———. "MacLennan's Rising Sun." Rev. of *The Watch*. *Saturday Night* 28 Mar. 1959: 29–31. Rpt. in Goetsch, *Hugh MacLennan* 119–22.

———. *The Manticore*. 1972. Markham: Penguin, 1983.

Djwa, Sandra. *The Politics of the Imagination: A Life of F.R. Scott*. Toronto: McClelland, 1987.

Dooley, D.J. "Hugh MacLennan: Everyman's Escape from the Waste Land." *Moral Vision in the Canadian Novel*. Toronto: Clarke, 1979. 79–92.

Useful discussion of moral and religious dimensions of *The Watch*.

Duncan, Dorothy. "My Author Husband." *Maclean's* 15 Aug. 1945: 7+.

Eliot, T.S. *The Complete Poems and Plays, 1909–1950*. New York: Harcourt, 1962.

Farmiloe, Dorothy. "Hugh MacLennan and the Canadian Myth." *Mosaic* 2.3 (1969): 1–9. Rpt. in Goetsch, *Hugh MacLennan* 145–54.

Contains interesting discussion of Part Five of *The Watch*.

Goetsch, Paul, ed. *Hugh MacLennan*. Critical Views on Canadian Writers. Toronto: McGraw, 1973.

Useful collection of reviews and articles.

———. "Too Long to the Courtly Muses: Hugh MacLennan as a Contemporary Writer." *Canadian Literature* 10 (1961): 19–31.

Includes discussion of *The Watch*.

Hancock, Geoff. *Canadian Writers at Work: Interviews with Geoff Hancock*. Toronto: Oxford UP, 1987.

Hirano, Keiichi. "Jerome Martell and Norman Bethune." *Studies in English Literature* [Tokyo] 44 (1968): 37–59. Rpt. in Goetsch, *Hugh MacLennan* 123–37.

A useful gathering of evidence, but critically naïve.

Hood, Hugh. *A New Athens*. Ottawa: Oberon, 1977.

James, Henry. *The Art of the Novel: Critical Prefaces*. Ed. R.P. Blackmur. 1934. New York: Scribner's, 1962.

James, William C. "A Voyage into Selfhood: Hugh MacLennan's *The Watch That Ends the Night*." *Religion and Culture in Canada/Religion et Culture au Canada*. Ed. Peter Slater. N.p.: Canadian Society for the Study of Religion, 1977. 315–32.

    An analysis of the novel from a religious perspective.

Keith, W.J. "Novelist of Essayist? Hugh MacLennan and *The Watch That Ends the Night*." In E. Cameron, *Hugh MacLennan: 1982* 55–63.

    Discusses the relation between fiction and non-fiction in connection with *The Watch*.

Kroetsch, Robert. "Hugh MacLennan: An Appreciation." In E. Cameron, *Hugh MacLennan: 1982* 135–39.

Lucas, Alec. *Hugh MacLennan*. New Canadian Library 8. Canadian Writers. Toronto: McClelland, 1970.

    Shrewd and perceptive overview of MacLennan's writing up to the time of publication.

Lynn, S. "A Canadian Writer and the Modern World." *Marxist Quarterly* 1.1 (1962): 36–43.

    A leftist critique of *The Watch*.

MacGregor, Roy. "A Voice out of Time." *Maclean's* 22 Sept. 1980: 45–48+.

    Interview at the time MacLennan published *Voices in Time*.

MacLennan, Hugh. *Barometer Rising*. 1941. New Canadian Library. Toronto: McClelland, 1961.

———. "Christmas without Dickens." *Mayfair* Dec. 1952: 45+. Rpt. in *The Other Side of Hugh MacLennan* 55–62.

    Contains an account of one of Dorothy Duncan's operations, parallelled in *The Watch*.

———. *Each Man's Son*. Toronto: Macmillan, 1951.

———. "The Future of the Novel as an Art Form." *Scotchman's Return and Other Essays*. Toronto: Macmillan, 1960. 142–58.

———. "Midsummer." *Thirty and Three*. Ed. Dorothy Duncan. Toronto: Macmillan, 1954. 12–25.

———. "New York, New York...." *The Montrealer* Mar. 1958: 28+. Rpt. in *The Other Side of Hugh MacLennan* 128–36.

———. *The Other Side of Hugh MacLennan: Selected Essays Old and New*. Ed. Elspeth Cameron. Toronto: Macmillan, 1978.

    Useful selection of MacLennan's non-fiction prose.

———. "Postscript on Odysseus." *Canadian Literature* 13 (1962): 86–87.

———. *The Precipice*. Toronto: Collins, 1948.

———. "Reflections on Two Decades." *Canadian Literature* 41 (1969): 28–39.

Rpt. in *The Other Side of Hugh MacLennan* 247–59.
An account of the writing of *The Watch* with comments on its historical context.
———. *Return of the Sphinx*. Toronto: Macmillan, 1967.
———. "The Story of a Novel." *Canadian Literature* 3 (1960): 35–39.
Personal account of the events surrounding the writing of *The Watch*.
———. *Two Solitudes*. Toronto: Collins, 1945.
———. "Victory." *The Other Side of Hugh MacLennan* 177–83.
A tribute to his first wife, Dorothy Duncan, written just after her death.
———. *Voices in Time*. Toronto: Macmillan, 1980.
———. *The Watch That Ends the Night*. 1959. Macmillan Paperbacks. Toronto: Macmillan, 1986.
———. "The Writer *Engagé*." *The Other Side of Hugh MacLennan* 269–87.
MacLulich, T.D. *Hugh MacLennan*. Twayne's World Authors Ser. Boston: Twayne, 1983.
Solid, general study. Chapter 5, "Requiem and Renewal," is devoted to *The Watch*.
Marshall, George O., Jr. *A Tennyson Handbook*. New York: Twayne, 1963.
Marshall, Tom. "Some Working Notes on *The Watch That Ends the Night*. *Quarry* 17.2 (1968): 13–16.
Mathews, Robin. "Ideology, Class, and Literary Structure: A Basis for Criticism of Hugh MacLennan's Novels." In E. Cameron, *Hugh MacLennan: 1982* 69–83.
The best of the ideological approaches to MacLennan's work.
McPherson, Hugo. "Fiction 1940–1960." *Literary History of Canada*. Ed. Carl F. Klinck. Toronto: U of Toronto P, 1965. 694–722.
Useful survey of MacLennan's fictional context.
Merivale, Patricia. "The (Auto)-Biographical Compulsions of Dunstan Ramsay." *Studies in Robertson Davies' Deptford Trilogy*. Ed. Robert G. Lawrence and Samuel L. Macey. English Literary Studies. Victoria: U of Victoria, 1980. 57–65.
A discussion of Canadian "elegiac romance" with useful comparison of Davies's *Fifth Business* with *The Watch*.
Metcalf, John. "Dear Sam." In Sam Solecki, John Metcalf, W.J. Keith, *Volleys*. Ed. J.R. (Tim) Struthers. Erin, ON: Porcupine's Quill, 1990. 35–70.
Morley, Patricia. *The Immoral Moralists: Hugh MacLennan and Leonard Cohen*. Toronto: Clarke, 1972.
Useful for its analysis of MacLennan's attack on puritan attitudes while himself retaining puritan values.
New, W.H. "The Apprenticeship of Discovery." *Canadian Literature* 29 (1966): 18–33.

Roberts, Ann. "The Dilemma of Hugh MacLennan." *Marxist Quarterly* 1.3 (1962): 58–66.
  Unsympathetic political critique of *The Watch*.
Ross, Malcolm. Rev. of *The Watch*. *Queen's Quarterly* 66 (1959): 343–44.
Ryerson, Stanley B. "Hugh MacLennan's View of Social Class and Nationhood." In E. Cameron, *Hugh MacLennan: 1982* 3–23.
Shek, Ben-Zion. "Commentary on Antoine Sirois." In E. Cameron, *Hugh MacLennan: 1982* 123–31.
Staines, David. "Commentary on W.J. Keith." In E. Cameron, *Hugh MacLennan: 1982* 64–68.
Tallman, Warren. "An After-Glance at MacLennan." Rev. of *The Watch*. *Canadian Literature* 1 (1959): 80–81.
Tener, Jean F., Sandra Mortensen, Marlys Chevrefils, comps. *The Hugh MacLennan Papers*. Calgary: U of Calgary P, 1986.
  Bibliographical; little material on *The Watch*.
Tennyson, Alfred. *Enoch Arden, etc.* London: Moxon, 1864.
Twigg, Alan. "Patricius–Hugh MacLennan." *For Openers: Conversations with 24 Canadian Writers*. Madeira Park, BC: Harbour, 1981. 83–96.
  Interview.
Whitman, Walt. *Leaves of Grass*. Philadelphia: McKay, 1900.
Woodcock, George. *Hugh MacLennan*. Studies in Canadian Literature. Toronto: Copp, 1969.
  General assessment. Chapter 10, "Odysseus Ever Returning," is devoted to *The Watch*.
———. *Introducing Hugh MacLennan's Barometer Rising*. Canadian Fiction Studies. Toronto: ECW, 1989.
———. "A Nation's Odyssey: The Novels of Hugh MacLennan." *Canadian Literature* 10 (1961): 7–18.
  Influential article, largely incorporated into Woodcock's *Hugh MacLennan*.
Yeats, W.B. "Dialogue of Self and Soul." *The Norton Anthology of English Literature*. 6th ed. Vol. 2. New York: Norton, 1993.
Zichy, Francis. "'Shocked and startled into utter banality': Characters and Circumstance in *The Watch That Ends the Night*." *Journal of Canadian Studies* 14.4 (1979–80): 90–105.
  An unsympathetic reading.

Index

Allan, Ted 77
Atwood, Margaret 86
Auden, W.H. 83–84

Barometer Rising (MacLennan) 21, 22, 27–28, 31, 32, 33, 44, 52, 75
Bethune, Norman 23, 76–77, 79, 85
Blake, William 16
Blodgett, E.D. 23, 45
Bonnycastle, Stephen 19, 24–25, 68, 96
Brazeau, Jacques 68
Buitenhuis, Peter 20, 21, 77, 88, 89
Bunyan, John 33, 80

Callaghan, Morley 57
Cameron, Elspeth 23–24, 36, 37, 38, 66, 72, 77, 83, 85, 95
Carlyle, Thomas 72
"Christmas without Dickens" (MacLennan) 36
Cockburn, Robert H. 20, 21, 23, 25, 36, 56, 59, 74

Davies, Robertson 19–20, 86, 94, 97–101
Dickens, Charles 36, 55, 56, 66, 70, 75, 86, 94
Dooley, D.J. 22, 66, 75, 89
Duncan, Dorothy 34, 35–36, 37, 38, 45, 57, 75, 90, 94

Each Man's Son (MacLennan) 31–32, 73
Eliot, T.S. 39, 68

Farmiloe, Dorothy 39, 68
Fielding, Henry 72
Findley, Timothy 14
Forster, E.M. 29, 40
Fosbery, C.S. 66
Franco, Gen. Francisco 65
Freud, Sigmund 53, 72–73
"Future of the Novel of an Art Form, The" (MacLennan) 14, 21

Gallant, Mavis 14
Goetsch, Paul 32, 90, 98
Gordon, Sidney 77

Hemingway, Ernest 46, 54, 61, 83
Hirano, Keiichi 23, 76–82, 91
Hitler, Adolf 53, 64, 65
Hodgins, Jack 101
Homer 31, 32
Hood, Hugh 58–59, 101

James, Henry 34
James, William G. 45
Jung, Carl 20, 98

Kroetsch, Robert 26

Laurence, Margaret 63, 87, 100
Lawrence, D.H. 29, 57, 86
Lucas, Alec 20, 21, 22, 56, 57, 58
Lynn, S. 23

MacGregor, Roy 37
MacLulich, T.D. 15, 22–23, 56
Marshall, Tom 24, 74

107

Mathews, Robin 23, 75, 79–80, 82
McPherson, Hugo 31, 88
Merivale, Patricia 93, 97, 99
Metcalf, John 86
Morley, Patricia 22, 82
Munro, Alice 86, 87
Mussolini, Benito 64, 65

New, W.H. 86
"New York, New York..."
 (MacLennan) 38–39

Precipice, The (MacLennan) 21
Proust, Marcel 19, 24, 29

"Reflections on Two Decades"
 (MacLennan) 15, 28, 29
Return of the Sphinx (MacLennan)
 21, 28, 53
Richler, Mordecai 68, 86
Roberts, Ann 23
Ross, Malcolm 17–18, 19, 20, 22
Ross, Sinclair 63
Roy, Gabrielle 68
Ryerson, Stanley B. 23, 67, 84, 85

Scott, F. R. 38, 57
Shakespeare, William 72
Shek, Ben-Zion 84–85
Spinoza, Benedict 24
Staines, David 47
Stalin, Josef 35, 64, 85

Tallman, Warren 18–19, 20, 21, 25,
 71, 94
Tennyson, Alfred 32, 51
Tillich, Paul 88
Tolstoy, Leo 13–14, 27, 29
Two Solitudes (MacLennan) 21, 28,
 68, 84

"Victory" (MacLennan) 36

Watts, Issac 43
Wiebe, Rudy 14, 86, 101
Woodcock, George 20, 21, 22, 31,
 39, 56, 84, 87, 101
Wordsworth, William 24
"Writer *Engagé*, The"
 (MacLennan) 28–29

Yeats, W.B. 59

Zichy, Francis 21, 25